SEXTASTIC!

Improve Your Love Life in Seven Weeks

Janalee Beck

BALBOA.
PRESS

A DIVISION OF HAY HOUSE

Balboa Press books may be ordered through booksellers or by contacting:

Balboa Press
A Division of Hay House
1663 Liberty Drive
Bloomington, IN 47403
www.balboapress.com
1 (877) 407-4847

Because of the dynamic nature of the Internet, any web addresses or links contained in this book may have changed since publication and may no longer be valid. The views expressed in this work are solely those of the author and do not necessarily reflect the views of the publisher, and the publisher hereby disclaims any responsibility for them.

The author of this book does not dispense medical advice or prescribe the use of any technique as a form of treatment for physical, emotional, or medical problems without the advice of a physician, either directly or indirectly. The intent of the author is only to offer information of a general nature to help you in your quest for emotional and spiritual well-being. In the event you use any of the information in this book for yourself, which is your constitutional right, the author and the publisher assume no responsibility for your actions.

Any people depicted in stock imagery provided by Thinkstock are models, and such images are being used for illustrative purposes only.
Certain stock imagery © Thinkstock.

Print information available on the last page.

ISBN: 978-1-5043-6843-8 (sc)
ISBN: 978-1-5043-6845-2 (hc)
ISBN: 978-1-5043-6844-5 (e)

Library of Congress Control Number: 2016917764

Balboa Press rev. date: 12/13/2016

To friends and family for their goodhearted and unwavering support:

R.D.S.
Sara Ann Mata
Angeline
S.L.G.
June Rose
Dr. Lee Yosowitz
Don "the wizard" Keas

CONTENTS

INTRODUCTION: WHAT YOUR MOTHER NEVER TOLD YOU

Hi, my name is Janalee Beck. My previous book, *How to Have Multiple Orgasms,* was about female sexuality. I received many letters from readers asking about the role of their partner in the process. Consequently, I felt compelled to write a follow-up workbook-style manual.

This book—*Sextastic! Improve your Love Life in Seven Weeks*—is for couples. My mission is to grow your capacity for intimacy and modify your style of communication, which heightens your sexual pleasure and creates more peaceful interactions. I also want to dispel numerous myths and misconceptions about romantic love. In short, I want to bring couples closer together.

The book shows couples how to gain intimacy. It also:

- Helps couples talk about sex and their feelings
- Explores ways to connect more passionately
- Strengthens cross-gender communication skills
- Boosts self-confidence in & outside the bedroom
- Helps readers overcome obstacles to oral sex
- Clarifies how lovers self-sabotage pleasure
- Offers 17 dynamic techniques for gratification
- Includes interactive exercises to build strong ties

I am an author, educator, entrepreneur, and wisdom-seeker. Some people say I talk about sex and orgasms the way other people talk about sneezes. I don't know if that's true or not, but orgasms and sneezes have a lot in common:

1. Both are natural.
2. Both are automatic reflexes.
3. Both are unpredictable.
4. Both result in feeling better when done right.

So, sneeze away! But please do so responsibly because promiscuous sneezing sometimes leads to physical and emotional consequences.

By taking a few hours of your time in the next seven weeks, you'll discover greater love, sex, romance, and intimacy for a lifetime. What a great trade-off! So you have everything to gain and nothing to lose. Be honest, kind, and gentle with yourself and your partner when completing exercises in this workbook to reap umpteen rewards.

Let the learning begin. Bring on the seven-week challenge!

How Couples Gain the Most
From this Workbook

Studies have shown that one week is the shortest time it takes to form a new habit, a fresh way of acting or being. Others report twenty-one days as the magical number. I've also heard forty. The truth is, establishing a new habit is individual-dependent. The activities, quizzes, and exercises are spread over seven weeks to ensure that you habituate what you learn. In any case, follow this workbook chronologically, and I predict you will see a positive difference in your romantic life. You will discover new ways to create, express, and receive loving words, touches, and actions.

Think of this book as a springboard to rekindle, refresh, and reboot your relationship. You can establish a supportive foundation for how to behave toward your partner in the future. The ultimate results are completely up to you. As a couple, are you willing to open up emotionally, share honest feelings, and explore new horizons?

Sextastic! is designed to get you on the right track and help you explore current areas of intimacy and heightened sexual pleasure. Follow the guidelines and discussions. Take the time to write down your answers. This process helps you realize that what you believe about sex and romance eventually becomes your reality. Throughout this journey, remember that love and affection are expressions of a mental mindset. Thought precedes feelings.

There's no perfect formula to enhance your intimacy, but this workbook steers you down the right road. Good luck!

> ## Great Sex is 90% Mental

Like most people, I've always been fascinated with how the mind works. It's one of the enduring unsolved mysteries. As a social worker for over ten years, I was always fascinated by psychology. Likewise, I learned about antecedents, behavior, and consequences. What precedes a sexual encounter (the antecedent) sets the stage for the actual sex event (the behavior), which ends up with both parties feeling better or worse (the consequence). To achieve the desired outcome, learn techniques and intimacy-enhancing tools to develop a better romance and achieve heightened sexual pleasure.

Here are a few essentials to maintain a healthy sexual relationship:

- Curiosity is always welcome.
- A bold desire for adventure is essential.
- Honesty is important.
- Letting go of preconceived notions is a must.

Many people self-sabotage their pleasure by not freeing up their minds to look at sex as a natural, healthy, and organic practice. Some have been brain-washed with restrictive religious beliefs. Others watch too much porn online. Adult movies, especially when watched together, can heighten the mood for couples.

However, if one party watches porn obsessively, he or she may have a misconception of what a normal loving relationship looks like, which then gets in the way of their reality. Relationships, and some marriages, crumble under such unrealistic expectations in the bedroom.

Most of us have been inspired briefly to be more loving and romantic by watching a movie, reading a book, or perhaps attending a pricey couples event. You may have been inspired short-term, but the motivation often doesn't stick very long. Do you ever wonder why? Here's a partial answer to this complicated question.

Memory for one thing. Your brain stores bits of information in a bunch of different places in the mind. You have to work hard to piece together what you want to retain. This workbook incorporates many learning modalities—visual, auditory, and kinesthetic—so you easily recall the messages and connect in a profound way.

The information in *Sextastic!* will foster long-term effects because the exercises are designed to reach you at a deeper, subconscious level. You don't just talk about an orgasm with your partner; you're both asked to draw one. You don't just practice a new technique with your spouse; you get direct feedback to trigger good feelings.

Hooray for taking the first step toward a lifetime of better intimacy! Get the sensual snowball rolling in a positive direction!

Kabrina:
The Woman Who Slept
With Three Generations Of Kings

Many years ago, I met an anthropologist who talked about ancient times like it was yesterday. He mentioned a woman, Kabrina, who was responsible for giving pleasure to three generations of kings. She must have been timeworn and wise when it came time to accommodate the last king. As the story goes, she was average-looking, yet radiant and fit. All three royals called her the 'favorite one.' Why? What was Kabrina's best-kept secret?

I have always been interested in stories that include sex-enhancing secrets. For instance, what did Kabrina do specifically? Would her secrets work for most women? And would they work for me?

Well, unfortunately, Kabrina's private sexual behaviors were never written down, although we have some pictures and written materials from antiquity about sex. Thankfully, I got the answers from my subconscious roughly a week after I heard the story. In the dark recesses of my cerebral cortex, I dreamt that Kabrina and I had a conversation while enjoying some goat cheese, sweet bread, and wine.

She represents the archetypal woman, the goddess in all of us. She was wearing a blood-red, powdery flowing dress that reached her ankles. She wore laced up leather shoes to her top of her calves. Sipping on my red wine, I asked Kabrina many questions that had preoccupied me over the past few days.

I looked into her old sage eyes and asked, "What's your secret for satisfying three generations of kings?" She chuckled. Kabrina then told me something I'll never forget as long as I live:

She whispered, "I have been a pleasure-giver for a very long time. At a very young age, I was selected for such activities because I had an unusual and beautiful mother who preceded me in the art of giving pleasure. It was not a choice I made for myself, yet I wouldn't have been happy doing anything else."

"Go on," I pleaded.

"You see, I was trained at an early age to trust my instincts and my body. I was taught to take care of myself, to walk upright and proud, to dance freely, and laugh frequently. I practiced exercises with the muscles surrounding my vagina. Eventually, I learned to watch for signs of excitement and arousal in myself before I even knew what that meant. I spent seven years in training before I ever experienced being naked with a king."

"Was your first time with a man difficult?"

"No, I suppose I was a little inept and perhaps a bit shy in the beginning."
She tilted her head as if remembering something. "I never pushed too far,
too fast. That was my mother's first rule of pleasure," Kabrina explained,
"and she guided me expertly. Sense the moment. Move gracefully. Breathe
deeply. Embrace the goodness in your partner."

"Did you love all three kings?" I interrupted.

Kabrina laughed. "I don't ever remember thinking about love. Whatever
happened, just happened. I accepted each king for who he was and reacted
to each one very differently. I followed my gut instincts, which were valued
by all the kings."

"And did you obey your instincts?"

"Yes. Strangely, when my youth faded, I reached new heights of ecstasy
with the third and final king."

"Hmm, why was that?" I asked.

"Well, you see," Kabrina continued, "I realized long ago that giving and
receiving pleasure is the same thing. My soul responds to the movements
of my body, and then I express my passion. I let my torso take the lead,
which opens up the warmth and desire in my heart."

"The third king showered me with attention. He would talk to me for
hours. We would watch the fire burn down, and he would play games with
me. I am always in the present with him. I am always enthusiastic about
him. There is nothing better in all the world than to be in his arms and he
knows it. I am not trying to please him. I am merely expressing what I feel
on the inside. His Majesty then responds with his goodness, his passion,
his instincts. That is all I know. You must discover this for yourself."

Poof.

In a flash, Kabrina disappeared along with my curiosity. Embracing these
life-affirming notions shaped my subsequent behaviors. It was all very Zen.

> **We please the most when we are not trying to please at all!**

To be in a happy place romantically means to open yourself up completely to the moment as if each night is the last time you'll ever make love. Imagine that for a minute. There's authenticity and real passion without any pretenses if you think it's your final drop of ecstasy.

The better your imagination, the better the sex. Who knows? On any given day, we can take our final breath. If it happens during a sexual encounter, so be it. Is there a better way to go?

Kabrina's secret is a powerful truth. To please the most, release your mind from the idea of seeking to please the other. Moment to moment, express the love you feel through gut-instinct movements, noises, and passion. When you find this for yourself, extraordinary sensations will follow automatically.

Express Your Natural Instincts To Crack the Code On Pleasure

Expressing natural instincts may sound easy. Usually, it takes a while to discover this secret for yourself. It's a process and doesn't happen overnight. *Sextastic!* will lead you in the right direction and help you figure out what recipe works best for you and your partner.

Of course, anyone can swipe left or swipe right and get a physical release and express the lust they feel. You can find sex day or night with the many social hook-up apps available. That isn't what this book is about, however.

When I discuss the emotional processes involved in passion, please think about a healthy relationship, not a one-night stand. At times I make general statements that are not true for everyone; nonetheless, I detect common patterns from observing and listening to others over time. For example, if you asked me who gets aroused more quickly—men or women—after looking at erotic pictures, the answer is another question: which man and which woman? In my opinion, that five-word question applies to every exercise in this book and nearly everything involving relationships.

Most men are visually stimulated before arousal. Women usually need a pleasant ambiance, a good conversation, or a sense of comfort in a relationship before expressing their inner passion. While getting aroused may be different for men than it is for women, the physiological signs are similar. It's easier to get on the same page as soon as you slow down your breathing, relax, and get in tune with the moment. As your breathing slows down, so will your partner's. Sharing intimacy with your lover should unfold naturally.

What gets men to express their true emotions is an ongoing connection to the physical. Isn't that the result women desire in the first place? Once you learn to get in tune with your natural instinct, you learn to feel the magical intensity of physical contact with a heightened sense of a connection. The results are phenomenal.

Kabrina truly cracked the code on pleasure. And so can you. Remember, attracting passion is nothing more than a mindset. It works for every woman because you were born with natural instincts that are genetically designed to flip on your physiological arousal triggers. It works like a charm.

Put Kabrina secrets to work, and you'll be astounded by the results. Practice embracing the moment. Breathe, relax, and never look back. Whenever you want real passion, just tap into your natural instincts and let nature take its course. Be an enthusiastic participant. Your partner will appreciate it.

The thing is, you don't have to change who you are a bit. Become sexually enlightened because of your openness to the idea. Be willing to try new things both by yourself and with your partner. Explore your body solo. It's a vital step in becoming open to sexual pleasure. Be willing to talk about your real needs with your lover.

Good communication doesn't happen overnight, but it will happen. Be prepared to show vulnerability, and you shall reap the rewards in sexual paradise!

Your partner will become a believer too! Soon, your partner might ask, "Wow, honey, what's up with you tonight? You were extraordinary! How did you do that anyway?"

"You motivate me" is always a nice comeback!

Six Winning Action Steps

Implement these six steps to enhance intimacy in your romantic relationship. Just to give you a heads-up, each weekly challenge will use a combination of the following types of exercises for an improved romantic partnership:

1: Answer the self-discovery quiz portion and use it as a springboard to greater intimacy. Better love, affection, and sex to some degree are based on how well you know yourself. Be truthful and direct with each other.

2: Say at least three relationship-enhancing declarations daily. You may have used affirmations in the past. It doesn't matter what you call them. Practice saying them out loud as instructed, twice a day.

3: Make Focused-Language, Intimacy Exchanges (F-L-I-E) a monthly habit. I recommend that these ten-minute sessions become a part of your routine. Many couples choose Sunday evening. These exercises build an ideal foundation to improve communication even in the best of relationships. It's a friendly and straightforward practice.

4: Jot down your feelings, thoughts, and ideas. You can use space in this workbook. Write in a separate notebook or personal journal if you prefer. Use it to check on your progress in three to six months. You'll be amazed at your growth throughout this journey.

5.   <u>Take action on the best-matched ideas for super results</u>. Again, what you practice each week can be a catalyst for great sex for the remainder of your relationship. Isn't it worth spending time implementing these steps for a lifetime of better love, romance, intimacy, and sex?

6:   <u>Positively reinforce good behavior in and outside the bedroom</u>. This workbook provides specific details to help you gain intimacy and passion in a variety of ways. So don't worry, it's all covered.

CHAPTER 1

WEEK ONE CHALLENGE: CREATING A HEALTHY RELATIONSHIP

It is essential that you agree not to have sex during the first seventy-two hours after you begin this challenge. Come on; you can wait a couple of days. There are reasons for this. Whether you've been together for a few months, a few years, or a few decades, it's important to build or rebuild a solid foundation. Trust the process.

Note: I will be using the following words interchangeably: spouse, partner, boyfriend, girlfriend, couple, and significant other, etc. Please apply your situation to the context while accepting the diversity of lovebirds in the world.

Take this self-discovery quiz. Document your answers. You will be asked to look back at these at the end of the seven-week challenge. For better results, believe in each other. There are no right or wrong answers. You won't be graded, I promise. Use this quiz as a springboard for discussion, and you'll uncover more insights over the next few hours (or days depending on the pace you choose).

Use the first three lines for his responses and the next few lines for hers. Respectfully, this also applies to same-sex partnerships, but I am going with these general terms for expediency. Use different colored inks. It may be easier when you look back later.

- Do you have a daily expectation of sexual contact from your partner?

His: _____

_____

_____

_____

_____

_____

Hers: _____

_____

_____

_____

_____

- Who is the initiator of the sexual affection most often?

His: _____

_____

_____

_____

_____

_____

Hers: _____

_____

_____

_____

_____

_____

- Do you understand the moods, feelings, and values of your mate?

His: _____

_____

_____

_____

_____

_____

Hers: _____

_____

_____

_____

_____

_____

- Would you rather be loved, appreciated, or understood? Why?

His: _____

_____

_____

_____

_____

_____

Hers: _____

_____

_____

_____

_____

- List three nonphysical characteristics you like about your partner?

His: _____

_____

_____

_____

_____

Hers: _____

_____

_____

_____

_____

- Do you believe your partner understands your core values?

His: _____

_____

_____

_____

_____

_____

Hers: _____

_____

_____

_____

_____

_____

- Are you optimistic that this workbook has the potential to help you? Why or why not? Will you be an active participant?

His: _____

_____

_____

_____

_____

_____

Hers: _____

_____

_____

_____

_____

_____

How Healthy Is Your Relationship?

Is your relationship R-I-P-E? This section helps readers discover how stable their current partnerships are when held to high standards. It explains how intimacy involves trust, humor, and communication. R-I-P-E is an acronym to describe a happy and mellow connection. A good partnership is:

R	=	Respectful
I	=	Intimate
P	=	Passionate
E	=	Emotionally-Supportive

Like a fine wine, a healthy relationship can be cultivated. For example, a red wine takes its sweet time before it's ready for consumption. Likewise, real companionship matures after a reasonable interlude. Love, at first sight, happens occasionally; but, realistically, it usually doesn't happen overnight. More and more, individuals are trying to discover what they did wrong in their last relationship. They don't want to blow it with their current mate. Be authentic. Let the partnership unfold naturally. If you try to rush it, you may blow it.

Attract a R-I-P-E Relationship!

R is for Respect: If there isn't mutual respect, you can kiss your romantic connection goodbye. When that goes, so does the love. Piece by piece, the sexual ardor you once shared disappears. A sculptor is extraordinary when she creates something out of nothing, but a disrespectful mate does the opposite. While we all lose our cool sometimes, nobody wants to live with criticism, put-downs, verbal abuse, or extreme negativity as a steady diet.

To gain self-esteem, you must first respect yourself. As Eleanor Roosevelt once said, and I'm paraphrasing here: other people can't insult you unless you give them permission. Practice being respectful.

If you disagree with your partner, explain the reasons behind your position. Share a story that reflects your point of view. Remember, multiple viewpoints can be right. In a nutshell, respect is a cumulative process. For a better connection, follow these four guidelines:

1. Ask questions every day. Discover your partner's thoughts, beliefs, feelings and impressions of life in general or about a particular topic. Figure out what your partner likes to do in and out of the bedroom. Let this unfold over time.

2. Listen to your partner. You don't have to agree with everything your partner says (that would be boring). Just understand what the other is saying and accept your partner's point of view. What makes the other tick? What events in your spouse's past make him or her act in a particular way?

3. Express your needs and desires. Be in tune with what makes you tick. Compromise when necessary. Use simple phrases. For more foreplay, express yourself. Be firm without demanding a particular outcome.

4. Be emotionally honest. A lack of honesty finds its way to the bedroom. This is a classic example of how a couple loses their sexual edge. One husband exclaimed, "We started out so passionate, but now my wife doesn't want anything to do with me!" If you are too passive, your partner may walk all over you. If you are too aggressive, you become an oppressive presence. Neither makes for a lasting romantic bond. The ideal is to strive for being assertive. State your position and move on. A sustained mutual respect is essential is a good relationship.

I is for Intimacy: Intimacy is a complex subject. In a good relationship, we seek out someone to balance our souls and stimulate our bodies. I interviewed clinical psychologist, Dr. Carolyn Goodrich of Edmond, Oklahoma about this challenging topic. "Consciously or unconsciously, most of us seek a partner with the same capacity for intimacy," says Dr. Goodrich. "A partner with greater intimacy scares us; one with too little bores us." Where do you stand in this delicate balancing act?

In my opinion, intimacy involves trust, humor, and communication. Without these three elements, the connection cannot survive long. Trust evolves over time. Real intimacy is only possible between trusting individuals. Without the assurance of your mate's faithfulness, you can never have true peace of mind (unless you have an open partnership or marriage). No judgments.

Unsurprisingly, humor plays a vital role as well. Remember, never take yourself too seriously. Adopt a playful mindset and life becomes your playground. Bring your sense of humor to the bedroom as well. I guarantee you'll need it someday. Your wit and banter should be free-flowing and easy to do with someone you love. If dialogue is a struggle, then reconsider why you're in the relationship in the first place. A happy partnership shouldn't be so much work that it's a continual struggle, although a little effort is needed in any relationship.

The other ingredient is healthy communication. As in most things, authentic rapport is the key to happiness in and outside the bedroom. Know what you need from a relationship and then develop the skills to ask for what you want. Chapter six covers gender-based communication styles in more depth. Listen to your partner and respond to his or her needs as best you can. A specific request, stated positively and paired with a positive tone of voice, usually gets good results.

In short, the quality of your communication fine-tunes the quality of your intimacy. The disparity between cross-gender communication styles is similar to the differences of those from contrasting cultural backgrounds. Sometimes the message gets lost in translation. For instance, a Californian may be put off by the manic gesturing and loud voice tone of an Italian New Yorker while he wonders why the west-coast guy is so quiet and non-responsive. (Doesn't he think my story is funny? Why hasn't he interrupted me or said anything?) It's a matter of a highly-involved style versus a highly-considerate way of communication. Again, these differences will be discussed further in chapter six as reported by a world-renowned linguist.

P is for Passion: Another element of a good relationship is passion. Dr. Bob Bohanske, a clinical psychologist in Mesa, Arizona, sums it up: "A passionate person is centered, unafraid of exposing who they are in any area...be it physical, political, humor...they express themselves and what they believe." If the attraction is solely based on lust, without mutual interests or goals, the relationship fades away sooner or later.

A couple can't predict compatibility upon first meeting, but two people can and frequently do feel a strong chemical attraction to each other at first sight. In some cases, this chemical reaction blossoms into mutual respect that enhances any sexual experience. It is not uncommon for a woman to focus on what the other person does for a living and his status. A woman might assume that if she finds someone who fits the image in her mind, then he or she must be the right person at the right time.

Some jump at the chance to go to bed with this so-called ideal partner, telling themselves they'll figure the rest out later. And sometimes you'll find a frog in bed with you. Sometimes you'll find a prince (or princess).

Bed-hopping may work for individuals who are not concerned with settling down. However, for women who want a commitment and a family, this approach rarely results in success. Males and females can find sexual passion with a multitude of partners if that's what they want. The fact is, great sex does not equal love. Sexual play without love can be a fun time, or it can be a hollow experience that leaves one or both people feeling exploited and lonely.

Dr. Bohanske suggests, "Passion should be self-motivated. It's best when sex is initiated because you crave and enjoy it—not done out of a sense of duty." Open yourself up to a romantic connection because you discover that your partner is caring, thoughtful, intelligent, and fun to be around. Both genders can enjoy sexual encounters without being in love. Sex-with-love, though, brings emotional satisfaction with an incredible intensity and a sweet vulnerability.

To achieve a close connection, learn to express your affectionate nature. Equally important is to share a similar level of passion. This allows each person to obtain a clear picture of his or her desires, which can lead to an understanding of the other partner's core values and a strong sense of self. Extraordinary passion stems from a deep-seated love. Cultivate a capacity for pleasure with your partner through encouragement and praise, not demands and critiques.

E is for Emotionally-Supportive: Some say women are nurturing and supportive by nature. There are plenty of men who have nourishing and caring personalities as well. As a general rule, do not expect your mate to replace your network of friends and vice versa. Instead, let your partner add texture to your support system. A loving partner bolsters your confidence when you need it. He celebrates your victories and is there to pick you up when you fail. Compassion, in most cases, can be re-learned by both men and women.

Resourceful couples work through their issues. Resolve problems as a couple. Periodically, it doesn't hurt to get advice from a trusted friend, family member, or therapist. Dr. Carolyn Goodrich explains, "A couple's level of commitment parallels their ability to support one another throughout the ups and downs of life." A relationship that unfolds in a natural way sets a foundation of communicating and accepting each other.

Commitment needs to ripen on its own. Never push. Out of emotional desperation, some people rush a good thing. Others put up barriers out of fears: fear of intimacy, fear of rejection, fear of vulnerability, and fear of abandonment. Counseling combined with meditation (and sometimes medication) can help resolve larger psychological issues.

There's no need to discuss every little concern with your partner. This becomes tiresome and drains your lover, who then becomes less likely to listen when more serious issues arise. Women can learn to hold back emotional insecurities periodically. A sensible man is ultimately attracted to a self-secure lady. Pick and choose what you share.

When support is chronically one-sided, the connection is doomed for failure. Honest people admit this failure and move on to find a partner who offers mutual respect, intimacy, passion, and emotional support. Cultivate your current relationship and it could ripen into a lifelong companionship!

Evaluate Your Partnership With A Self-discovery Quiz:

To score this quiz, give yourself one full point if you answered <u>Yes</u>, ½ point for <u>Sometimes</u> or <u>Depends</u>, and zero points for answering <u>No</u>. While a written test cannot determine if your love connection is healthy, take this quiz to discover if you and your partner are on the right path for a healthy relationship:

Do you feel your partner respects you as a whole, complex individual whose sum is greater than the parts?
Yes ( ) No ( ) Sometimes ( ) Depends ( )

Would you trust your partner if he or she travels with an attractive colleague for business purposes?
Yes ( ) No ( ) Sometimes ( ) Depends ( )

Do you laugh together throughout the week and not just when you're out drinking or with friends?
Yes ( ) No ( ) Sometimes ( ) Depends ( )

Are you able to share your most private thoughts, ideas, dreams, impressions of life and feel your spouse listens?
Yes ( ) No ( ) Sometimes ( ) Depends ( )

Do you want to please and be pleased in the bedroom? (Is your sex life a balanced, happy one?)
Yes ( ) No ( ) Sometimes ( ) Depends ( )

Do you feel the urge to communicate everyday experiences with your mate?
Yes ( ) No ( ) Sometimes ( ) Depends ( )

Do songs, movies, or books carry more meaning for you because of your relationship? Do you sometimes feel sentimental about a particular song?
Yes ( ) No ( ) Sometimes ( ) Depends ( )

Would you support your spouse's efforts and dreams even if you didn't agree with the practicality of what he wants to do?
Yes ( ) No ( ) Sometimes ( ) Depends ( )

Does the sound of your boyfriend or girlfriend's voice comfort you?
Yes ( ) No ( ) Sometimes ( ) Depends ( )

Do you have a warm, cozy feeling inside when cuddling? Do you feel extra secure when together?
Yes ( ) No ( ) Sometimes ( ) Depends ( )

Your Quiz Results:

If you answered a resounding yes to all ten questions, get real. Nobody's that perfect. Just kidding, your partner sounds fantastic. Perhaps you've been together for a long time, or it could be the start of a meaningful connection.

If you gave an affirmative answer to at least eight questions, bravo! Your partner is a keeper. You have more going for you than most couples. Affirmative answers to 6-7 questions demonstrate a long-term connection is likely, and it is a definite sign that real love looms ahead.

If you responded optimistically to 4-5 questions, then you're in a development stage. Your partnership may not have had enough time to ripen, or you've been together so long that at least one party doesn't care anymore. You can still work your way to a better connection. Remember, don't push it. Let it unfold naturally. If you feel like it's a constant struggle to bond on a deeper level, however, perhaps you need to re-evaluate the situation.

Now if you said yes to only 1-3 questions, then it's probably time to move on down the road. There are other fish in the sea. Life's too short to waste your precious time and energy. After ninety days without your partner around, your brain is wired to release emotional attachment to both the good and the bad times. Memories become foggy. Usually, this makes it easier to move on. Turn the relationship into a platonic one if the friendship warrants it. Sooner or later, you'll start seeing someone else with a greater potential for good compatibility.

Icebreaker Activity For Couples

Yes, I'm going to ask you to draw a couple of pictures. It'll be fun! Happily, you won't be graded on the quality of your artwork. Read the specific instructions before you start drawing. I want you to complete the following:

1. Draw a picture of an <u>ORGASM</u>. (If you've never had one, just imagine.)
2. Use images, shapes, or symbols, but no letters or numbers.
3. Be spontaneous.
4. Pretend you're showing this picture to a creature from another planet, an alien or someone who doesn't understand language as we know it. You are desperate to communicate the concept.

In the space provided or on separate pieces of paper, take roughly two to five minutes to draw your masterpiece. Let one person draw first, making sure you cover up your partner's picture with a piece of paper. Then, unveil both drawings at the same time.

Her Orgasm Drawing:	His Orgasm Drawing:

Isn't it fun to see what the other person drew? Were they similar in any way? Different? Do you think the differences are based on gender or only based on the personality type of person drawing?

Take several minutes to share your thoughts with your partner. Let's start with the woman's picture first. The man becomes the observer and talks about what he sees, how it makes him feel, what comes to mind etc. The artist responds by saying if it's close to the mark, off-base, or gets straight to the heart of your intention. Talk. Laugh. Giggle. Have fun.

Okay, now switch. The female now becomes the observer.

Here's a drawing change-up. This time, draw <u>LOVE</u>. Make a picture of the concept. Again, do not think. Draw the first thing that comes to your mind. Do not use any letters. Use only images and symbols. Pretend you're showing this to someone from outer space. Who knows? You may be doing just that (ha ha).

Her Love Drawing:	His Love Drawing:

Individuals are predominantly the left-brain (more logical) or the right-brain (more creative) type. That's not to say we can't use both sides of our brain. Apparently, we cross over and use them when we need to. You choose to draw what feels natural. Again, one person becomes an observer first. What differences or similarities did you see?

When a group of women completed this exercise at my seminar, we passed our drawings around the circle. You should have heard the exclamations and chuckles. The most common element we found was that nearly everyone used a symbol for the orgasm picture. However, seminar participants drew a picture consisting of two or more people when asked to portray the concept of love. What did you discover?

Hooray! It's Time To Celebrate!

Show your appreciation for taking the time to move forward toward love, romance, intimacy, and better sex. It's time to reinforce each other. It's usually the women who purchase books like these. So if your boyfriend took the time to share a few intimate moments with you, reinforce him.

At the risk of sounding a little woo-woo (mystical), color visualization works. Imagine surrounding your loved one with a soothing green or gold light while you touch. Be creative and make the light swirl around, say head to toe. Perhaps change colors in the middle or have colors move from the head and out the vagina (or penis). After a few minutes or so, ask your partner if they feel a different sensation. You might be surprised. Try this when you're watching T.V. together and see if your partner notices it.

Instead of a back massage, does your mate want an arm or a leg rub down? Perhaps a foot rub? Some people enjoy a hand massage. A few minutes is enough this time, but please don't rush the process. That's a turn-off.

The receiver decides if he wants his treat with or without lotion/baby oil. It's an added pleasure if you warm up the baby oil first. Not too hot. Try a dot on your wrist, like you're testing the milk in a baby bottle. The receiver also is accountable for feedback such as, "Oh, that feels terrific." or "Hmm, baby, you're the greatest."

Remember, specific feedback is always preferred: "I like it when you use deep pressure and rotate my fingers from side to side." Now, switch places. The receiver becomes the giver. Spend the next ten to fifteen minutes showering each other with warm loving light and affection. Try something uncommon today.

Be proud of yourselves for sticking with a program to improve your relationship. If you followed my early instructions, you've waited roughly seventy-two hours to have sex. Did you pass the test? Anticipation creates romantic airs. Today's the day!

Super Job! You've completed
Week One Challenge:
Creating a Healthy Relationship

CHAPTER 2

WEEK TWO CHALLENGE: MOVING TOWARD INTIMACY

Are you moving toward or away from intimacy?

As individuals, we are moving closer to our goals and dreams, or we are moving away from them. If you are drinking water, you are moving closer to a healthy body. If you are eating a burger and fries, you are moving away from one. Eating nothing is closer to your goal. There is no twilight-zone-like, neutral state where we are not moving toward or away from a destination. Every moment, theoretically, we choose to walk toward or away from something.

The same goes for couples. Every minute you're together, each of you makes a choice. Is it a wise or an unwise choice? Ask yourself:

> **Am I behaving in a respectful, loving manner right now?**

As you know from chapter one, intimacy is a close bond, an energy exchanged between two people. We are attracted to others for lots of reasons, especially those who have a similar level or need for emotional

17

connecting. Intimacy is a full condition that embraces trust, honest communication, and a sense of humor.

To be sure, you feel an intimate moment before you realize it is happening. Conversation flows freely one minute, leads to laughter, and then moves smoothly to pure silence, being in the same quiet space while still connected.

Take the Following Intimacy Discovery Quiz:

1. How often do you feel intimate with your mate?
2. What does intimacy mean to you?
3. Do you feel intimate at the movie theater and the lake?
4. Does your level of intimacy match your spouse's?
5. Do you feel suffocated by your partner's behavior?
6. Are you satisfied with your current level of intimacy?
7. Is it harder to feel intimate outside of the bedroom?

Jot Down Your Thoughts & Impressions:

His: _____

_____

_____

_____

_____

_____

Hers: _____

_____

_____

_____

_____

_____

What is a Focused-Language Intimacy-Exchange?

Are you ready for the single most useful tool to move closer as a couple? It's a simple ten-minute activity per person. You're both going to engage in a brief activity—a Focused-Language Intimacy-Exchange (F-L-I-E)–that can be accomplished easily anytime. You may like it so much you'll tell your friends to try it. For good results, practice it once a month or so. No need to overdo it, though. Otherwise, it becomes a chore rather than a positive experience.

Often, a lack of communication is where the trouble in paradise begins. Couples forget the art of listening. We forget to look at each other and only listen. When conversing with a new friend, we often take the extra energy to be attentive to their stories. Since we know our partner so well, we think we can predict what they will say, and therefore we don't have to listen. Well, that's not true. We're complex beings. We're thinkers, not our past thoughts. We evolve. We grow. We learn. We transform.

A Focused-Language Intimacy-Exchange (F-L-I-E) is intended for the purpose of awareness and transformation. Try to pay attention to the information you are receiving during the next week. Take one small step. No significant changes. Subtle small steps lead to greater intimacy in the long run.

You can't read your partner's mind no matter how emotionally close you are to that person. Sure, it's okay to wonder what the other person is thinking about once in a while. It's an endless nonsensical game to ask your partner, "A penny for your thoughts?"

Perhaps the other person is not thinking much of anything except that they want a turkey sandwich. Realize there's no benefit in discussing where you stand in the relationship all the time either. In fact, most men and many women simply want to enjoy a relationship—not analyze it to death. This exercise will break the dubious cycle of analysis.

F-L-I-E is a ten-minute activity for couples. Even for the quiet or shy, it's simple to do. It's also remarkably effective. Let me introduce one version of it. Flip a coin to see who goes first. Let's say the woman begins. She will ask three simple questions. You can make up your questions later. Ask these:

1. On a scale from 1-100, where do you see our intimacy level?
2. Where would you like it to be (on the same scale)?
3. What can I do to help move us from a_____to _____?

Use whatever words makes you feel the most comfortable. For instance, you might say, "Hey, babe, what can I do to help us go from a seventy-five to a ninety-five?" Now, stop and listen.

It's crucial that you strictly follow these rules during a F-L-I-E session. The rules here are simple, but simple is not always easy.

> Rule #1: The Questioner may not TALK.**
> Rule #2: The Questioner may not ARGUE.
> Rule #3: The Questioner may not CRITICIZE.
> Rule #4: The Questioner may not INTERRUPT.
> Rule #5: The Questioner may not GIVE EXCUSES.

**You may hold up your hand, classroom style, and ask a clarifying question, such as "Can you give me an example?" as long as you use a neutral tone of voice.

The questioner's job is to listen, absorb, and learn!

Okay, now it's time to reverse roles. Each person only takes about four to five minutes to state how they could feel more intimate. This F-L-I-E exercise is intended to be a quick and lighthearted activity, yet it's an important way to communicate one's needs without making the other person feel attacked or criticized. Please keep the purpose in the forefront of your mind—to be more connected, appreciated, and loved.

For this to work, both you and your significant other must stick to the rules. Once you comprehend your partner's wishes, apply it to your daily routine. Your partner should absorb what you said and then use it when applicable. When you notice a behavioral transformation, tell your partner how much you appreciate the fact that he listened to you. And vice versa.

This exercise is designed to be the opposite of a drawn-out bitch session. Nobody enjoys criticism. A language exchange is a better approach to greater intimacy and a sense of deeply-rooted bonding.

Complete the F-L-I-E Exercise

You've heard the expression, "Less is more." Well, it applies here. Once the exercise is complete, please do not sit around and analyze your partner's answers. Just absorb it. Process at a later time. Men crave less talk, more action. Generally speaking, do activities you both enjoy and your intimacy will grow by leaps and bounds.

Processing usually takes a few days to sink in. Let your partner's words simmer in your brain. Something positive blooms from this activity more often than not. Slip this activity into your monthly routine. Watch your level of closeness grow. This beats nagging, arguments, or endless discussions every time a conflict arises.

Put On Your Calendar Today!

What time of day is most convenient for both of you to complete this ten-minute Focused-Language Intimacy-Exchange? Does morning or night work best?

_____

_____

What day of the week is best? You might select the third Sunday of every month:

Monday ☐ Tuesday ☐ Wednesday ☐
Thursday ☐ Friday ☐ Saturday ☐ Sunday ☐

_____

_____

Jot down your impressions of this activity. How might you personalize this to better meet your needs? You are the co-directors of your relationship. Be creative and let the good times roll!

His: _____

_____

_____

_____

_____

_____

Hers: _____

_____

_____

_____

_____

_____

All healthy partnerships want to feel connected, so stay tuned-in to each other. What are some ways to accomplish that specifically? If you've never heard of affirmations or declarations, no worries. It's simply a statement you read, say to yourself, or say out loud on a regular basis.

Many people learn about affirmations through self-improvement books or motivational seminars; others practice with a like-minded spiritual group. Psychologists and therapists find them to be useful tools. Professional athletes, amateur sports enthusiasts, and physical trainers integrate written and verbal affirmations to increase confidence and create positive belief systems.

Affirmations will help rewire your brain when you practice them on a regular basis. Use my examples of relationship-enhancing declarations until you're ready to make up your own. Have fun with it. This works:

1. Select a time for this two-minute activity each day.
2. Write out one to four affirmations on a sticky note.
3. Tape your handwritten note on your mirror.
4. Repeat them while doing your morning a nighttime routine.

My suggestion is simple. Do this once in the morning when you fix your hair or brush your teeth and then again before bed during your nightly ritual. According to some of the best motivational speakers, repeat your affirmations—aka Relationship-Enhancing Declarations—five times each twice a day. For better results, write them in your personal affirmation notebook. Switch up the phrasing to suit yourself. Practice these out loud and with feeling!

Left-Brained:	Right-Brained:
1. I accept my partner _____ (name) for who he/she is.	1. I accept _____ (name), my eternal companion, because I am brimming over with love and affection.
2. I accept you. I accept me. I allow you to accept me.	2. I choose to be an accepting person of others and myself because I choose mercy over justice.
3. I forgive my partner for any and all past, present, and future slip-ups.	3. I forgive my partner easily. I want to express unconditional love, support, and devotion.
4. I forgive you. I forgive me. I allow you to forgive me.	4. I choose to be forgiving of others and myself because I would rather be compassionate than judgmental.

You may not notice a difference at first, but these powerful messages are playing tapes in your mind. By the sixth or seventh week, for example, some of the messages will actualize and become a habit. You can change your affirmations after a one or two months. Do what feels right. Be comfortable. Write your own. Enjoy the results.

The next time your spouse does something irritating, you'll automatically forgive him or her more quickly. Your subconscious mind wants to be forgiving and forgiven. Sometimes, you are the annoying one. Remember, nobody's perfect. You'll become more accepting and tolerant. As we admire more and criticize less, our relationship is bound to be happier, more peaceful, and more loving.

Consequently, we become more attractive. Spiritually speaking, what you put out in the world, you receive. It's Karma. Like the old saying goes: "To receive love, you must give love."

Create Your Own Relationship-Enhancing Declarations

Start with yourself. Think of one or two small habits that you want to break. Perhaps something that irritates your partner. What is the best solution to avoid a potentially harmful situation? Write down a phrase that matches your personality.

Left-Brained:	**Right-Brained:**
1. _____	1. _____
_____	_____
2. _____	2. _____
_____	_____
3. _____	3. _____
_____	_____

State them using positive language. Don't write, "I choose to stop arguing about X." Instead write, "I opt to speak in a conversational tone when X happens." Or: "I choose to hand the remote control to my wife when she asks for it." Think about the outcome you desire. A calmer inner mind? A peaceful household? No screaming?

Learn to accept minor flaws in our partner. When we admit our many imperfections, we become grateful for the love we receive in spite of them. Remember the biblical verses about taking the log out of our eye before trying to remove the speck in the other. (Matthew 7:1-5)

Create Affirmations For Your Partner:

Okay, now that you've got the idea and you're feeling brave, why not create one or two uplifting Declarations/Affirmations for each other?

Your partner may be aware of an area in which you need to have more self-confidence or self-esteem. Such statements are a way to send explicit messages to your mind. Be gentle. Lovingly write a couple of affirmations that will uplift and support each other:

| **Affirmations for Her:** | **Affirmations for Him:** |

1. _____   1. _____

  _____   _____

2. _____   2. _____

  _____   _____

Relationship-Enhancing Declarations:

Left-Brained:	Right-brained:
1. I am worthy of being loved.	1. I am the light of love shining brightly, bringing joy and affection to all I meet.
2. My love is great and real.	2. My love overflows from the inside out and I find it easy to express at all times.
3. I choose to be lovable.	3. I am a lovable gift of God—content and kindhearted throughout the day.

See. That wasn't too difficult. The hard part is to continue a version of this practice often. A short daily routine enhances your chances for success in any area of your life, including your sex life.

One of the most important ways to keep your passion alive is caring for your partner the same way you want to be cared for. Amazing how well the 'Golden Rule' works! Concentrate on the positives in your relationship and why you fell in love in the first place. Perhaps the the best option is to accept your boyfriend or girlfriend and don't try to change him or her.

Great! You just completed
Week Two Challenge:
Moving Toward Intimacy

CHAPTER 3

WEEK THREE CHALLENGE: FOSTERING THE RIGHT MENTAL MINDSET

Ways to Open Up Before, During, or After Sex

There is a host of ways to get the right mental mindset. Try some of the following methods to channel a romantic spirit:

1. Look at your partner's facial features when you make love. Study his or her face carefully at other times. What expressions do you love the most?

2. Think about a waterfall or beautiful scenery, perhaps places you've visited or a location you've seen in a movie.

3. Go to your cheerful safe place. Do you lean toward a space at home or do you head outdoors?

4. Image your bodies meshing into a unifying ball of green and white light. Choose any color. Now swirl a favorite color around your partner's body. Start at the top and move downward or vice versa.

5. Visualize a celebrity crush. (Don't reveal this if your partner is the jealous type. Some things are better left unsaid.) Sir Lancelot is a reliable fantasy stand-in.

Sometimes it's fun to create a self-script during sex. Say how much you love him or her, but not out loud. Express your feelings silently. You will convey the meaning. Continually tell yourself how much pleasure you give your partner. What a superb romantic god or goddess you are becoming!

Pretend to be a different person. Become an actor, sort to speak, and decide what accent you might use. Become a character in one of your favorite movies. What's your motivation in this scene? Use comic relief, "You Tarzan, me Jane!"

Listen! Sing! Move! Touch!

Take a few minutes to select a song or piece of music that resonates with both of you. My heart melts when I see a couple look into each other's eyes and say, "Aah, they're playing our song." It's very sweet.

You may already have a song picked out. Perhaps you selected a favorite song from your wedding. Many lovers remember what song was playing when they kissed for the first time or when they fell in love or when X happened. Love songs produce goosebumps to lovers around the world.

Think about it. There's no rush. Let each person pick out a few songs that remind them of the other person. The goal is to decide on a tune that captures your essence as a couple or that sends chills up your spine. Got it?

Write the name of the tune(s) below:

His: _____

_____

_____

_____

_____

_____

Hers: _____

_____

_____

_____

_____

_____

Why did you select these tunes? Now it's time to play the song. Simply get comfortable and listen to the song together. Say nothing the first time and do not touch. You can laugh. You can dance. You can look at each other. Let the music touch your heart.

Create Positive Anchors (Emotional links)

For practical reasons, an anchor and an emotional link will be used interchangeably in this chapter. Anchoring—in neuro-linguistic programming—refers to the process of association at the peak of a highly charged state, usually an internal response to an external trigger, like a song or a touch or a smile. It means there is a tendency for one element of an intense experience to bring back the entire experience. We naturally link things that happen to us.

Sometimes we have a negative response, which is triggered by an external source. For example, the sound of sirens with flashing lights reminds us that a cop wants to pull us over and our heart rate increases. When we realize it's an ambulance, our racing heart slows back to normal.

A rich, intense experience helps solidify the emotional link. A touch on your wrist may trigger a sexual fantasy. A voice tone or particular phrase can become an anchor for a boost of confidence. For an anchor to remain strong, it needs to be reinforced. When we deliberately set up an anchor, we can accidentally neutralize its power. It's a sophisticated process, but I will walk you through an example.

Don't worry. We're not doing a research project here. We only want to create a personal emotional link between you and your partner to use anytime. Once you get a warm and fuzzy, intense feeling, you can then create an emotional link between you and your partner. To create this, you'll each need to think of ways to express yourself, ways that you cherish:

- A word or phrase NOT used in normal conversation
- An unusual tone of voice or unique accent
- A simple physical sign of affection
- A smile or a wink

Follow these instructions for a one-of-a-kind positive trigger you create:

1. Listen to the tune you choose above for a second time together.
2. When your emotions are the most intense, like during a favorite verse or crescendo in the song, I want you to do two things simultaneously:
   a. Say your distinct phrase, such as 'pink elephant', or repeat a favorite movie phrase, using a funny voice or a made-up accent.
   b. Touch your mate in a distinct way, like two squeezes of his left wrist with the palm of your hand. Pull her index finger gently. Scratch lightly just above the ear. Cup your partner's elbow. It's best to choose something you can use in a public place. Something you don't normally do.
3. Now smile or wink.

You have now consciously created an auditory, kinesthetic, and visual link between the intense emotional mood and your partner. You have created a solid anchor with a word, a touch, an accent, and a smile. It's important to link the two actions during a time when you're feeling loved and connected. Otherwise, you may be connecting a negative emotion.

How Do I Use This Anchoring Technique To Create A Trigger?

An anchor can become a useful tool for self-empowerment for helping stimulate creativity or learning to concentrate better or promoting sexual feelings. Used intermittently, you can trigger a warm fuzzy feeling by simply saying the distinctive word or phrase and then touching your partner in the unusual manner chosen above.

Like anything else, if overused, an anchor can lose its effectiveness. We can become desensitized to even if it's positive. It has to be reinforced and used now and then when a situation arises that warrants it.

Your new emotional-link can now be used as a trigger when you're at the movies, a party or a restaurant together, like a secret language. A verbal trigger can be used over the phone. If you are out with friends, try fitting 'pink elephant' in your conversation as an insider's joke, which is always intimate and fun.

Negative Anchor:	Positive Anchor:
If someone you love has been involved in a medical emergency, the sounds of an ambulance siren may cause your heart rate to increase for months or even years afterwards.	You attend a very memorable party, have a few beers, and meet someone simpatico named Jake who taps you on the back in a friendly manner.
These sounds trigger memories of the traumatic incident and incite unfavorable emotions. You may even have symptoms of PTSD for a while after a death-defying event.	Months later, a happy state is triggered when you hear the name Jake or when someone else pats you in a similar fashion. You may never connect the two events on a conscious level, but your mood has improved.

Be careful. Negative anchors can be created as well. The nearly-universal example is when parents call a child by his full name when they are about to reprimand him. When a boy hears, "Timothy Tim Thompson," he automatically freezes, thinking he's in trouble—even if he happens to be thirty years old. Not a good practice. Parents unintentionally create a negative and lasting cognitive downbeat link. Hearing our full given name should make us smile, not frown.

Anchoring emotional links can be created inadvertently when we are in some altered state due to drugs or alcohol, insomnia, sensory-deprivation, or deep meditation. We also create anchors, consciously or unconsciously, when we are involved in a highly-charged ripe moment or an intensely painful one.

For example, when I was twelve years old, I drank so much grape punch that I got nauseous and threw up. To this day, I cannot consume grape drinks because the smell makes me feel sick to my stomach. Of course, it's possible to retrain our minds and learn how to de-link ourselves with practice. If I wanted to, I could re-introduce grape drinks into my diet, using these anchoring techniques.

For a loving couple, this anchoring method can also be used to boost confidence or share warm feelings. You now have a distinct way to be in charge of uplifting emotions. Create links and then pull the trigger. When you're riding together in the car, just reach over and touch your partner in that unique way. Let the fun and fantasies begin.

He may not even know why he's feeling warm and fuzzy inside all of a sudden. Across a room full of people, use your trigger phrase and smile. It works like magic. And it's one of the best little secrets to keeping a healthy relationship alive!

Commit to some quality time with your partner doing something you both enjoy. Fun activities like going to the movies at the cinema, taking long walks with your dog, or having a picnic in the backyard are perfect opportunities to strengthen your secret anchors. You'll see great results!

Female Fireworks

Yes, this book is about sex and relationships. But it's even more about displaying loving behaviors outside of the bedroom. We all know, instinctively, that good sex goes hand-in-hand with internal moods, attitudes, and behaviors.

In 1995, a friend of mine introduced me as 'the sex author' at her workplace and many of her colleagues were eager to get my opinion about their love life. One woman yanked me into her office and shut the door. She burst out, "I've been married five years and I love my husband. Why does it take me so long to get warmed up for sex? Kurt gets frustrated and says he feels unmanly because he has to work so hard just to get me in the mood. He wonders if I still love him. Of course I do. Please, Janalee, help me!" Her husband got very frustrated. It takes many women thirty to ninety minutes to transition to the feminine mode after work. Sometimes it's just a timing issue. All I could say on short notice was to:

- Learn more about your body.
- Practice arousal triggers by yourself.
- Show your spouse what you like: the more details, the better.
- Use a variety of ways to transition from work mode to home mode.
- Try warming yourself up before a lovemaking session.
- Invite your husband in when you're ready.

Every woman needs to discover what pleases her and what doesn't. Then, she needs to find out what pleases her partner and what doesn't. A self-discovery journey begins with a single step. The woman mentioned above called me a few weeks later to say, "Thank you. You helped save my marriage! And my husband sends his appreciation, too." Her gratitude so moved me that it lead me to a greater passion for sharing feminine secrets.

Love Is A Mental Mindset

Love is a frame of mind. Treat your partner the way you want to be treated. That's the Golden Rule. You want them to be honest with you. You want to be appreciated. You want to be valued. You want to be respected. Mirror those behaviors and respond with gratitude when these attributes are reciprocated.

Nobody likes to be taken for granted. It is easy to fall into the trap of misbehaving with our loved ones. Sometimes it seems easier to be nice toward outsiders because there are no strings attached. You don't have any emotional baggage with strangers or acquaintances.

If you live together, it's crucial that you and your partner act in respectful ways and apologize when you make mistakes. Some men apologize indirectly with flowers or a simple declaration, "It won't happen again." Even if your spouse rarely says the actual words, "I'm sorry," he still feels bad about his behavior.

Clearly, it's important to establish boundaries at the beginning of a relationship. Stand up for yourself. If you feel disrespected, explain why. Share a story about how a similar thing happened to you in the fifth grade and why this upsets you so much.

Set up rules for disagreements and discuss consequences ahead of time so no party is left scratching their head. Communication styles are covered more in depth in chapter six.

Explore Practical Ways To Connect

1. Does atmosphere turn-on you and your partner? Think about your physical surroundings, lighting, music, etc. What do you smell? What do you see? What do you sense around you? Make a list here of what you like.

His: _____

_____

_____

_____

_____

_____

Hers: _____

_____

_____

_____

_____

2. Have you tried any sort of relaxation techniques? There are hundreds of books on the subject of stress reduction, meditation, and breathing exercises. Yoga and affirmations help clear the mind and create balance. (See my suggested list below at the end of this challenge.) Think. Talk. Check out websites. Now, decide on at least two to three action steps you are going to take in this area:

His: _____

_____

_____

_____

_____

_____

Hers: _____

_____

_____

_____

_____

_____

3. Do you like spontaneity or do you prefer a schedule? If you like to know that you're going to have sex on certain days of the week, when? (Discuss a compromise, if needed.)

His: _____

_____

_____

_____

_____

_____

Hers: _____

_____

_____

_____

_____

4. Could you perk up your routine by role-playing or sex toys?

His: _____

_____

_____

_____

_____

Hers: _____

_____

_____

_____

_____

5. What new activity would you both be comfortable trying at least once?

His: _____

_____

_____

_____

_____

Hers: _____

_____

_____

_____

_____

_____

6. Do you need some "transitional time" after work or after putting your children to bed? Do you want a chance to unwind separately? For how long?

His: _____

_____

_____

_____

_____

_____

Hers: _____

_____

_____

_____

_____

7. What time-honored things to you like to do before or after making love? Do you want to try something new or change anything?

His: _____

_____

_____

_____

_____

_____

Hers: _____

_____

_____

_____

_____

A Few Fun-filled Ideas

Make a list of fun activities you enjoy doing at home side-by-side. Then post it on the refrigerator:

- Relax in a hot tub
- Play cards
- Massage (or reflexology)
- Do a crossword puzzle
- Watch Netflix
- Read in bed together
- Mind games (online)
- Play a word game
- Walk barefoot outside (grounding)
- Eat a light meal before, during, after sex?
- Listen to your favorite playlist

8. Does a change of venue help get you in a romantic mood? List places that you both agree on as being a romantic setting.

His: _____

_____

_____

_____

_____

_____

Hers: _____

_____

_____

_____

_____

_____

9. When is the next time you can schedule a visit to a particularly romantic spot? Plan a getaway. Who's in charge of making the plans? (If money is tight, you could switch homes with some dear, trusted friends who don't live far away. It's a change of scenery for both. It's like a free vacation.)

Plans for a Romantic Getaway:

_____

_____

_____

_____

_____

Write Down Creative Ideas about Getting into the Right Mental Mindset:

1. _____

_____

2. _____

_____

3. _____

_____

Supercharge your thoughts, feelings, and actions. Your words will trigger positive movement in the bedroom!

Way to Go! You've Completed
Week Three Challenge:
Fostering the Right Mental Mindset

CHAPTER 4

WEEK FOUR CHALLENGE:
EXPLORING BELIEFS
AND CORE VALUES

Determine what the following statements conjure in your mind. Obviously, some of them are not entirely true or false. As usual, the reality lies somewhere in between. When people say there are two sides to every story, they're dead wrong. There are always three sides: yours, mine, and the truth (ha ha). Rare is the statement that is 100% black-and-white truth.

Obviously, gradations of truth depend upon our perspective. My wish is that this exercise leads couples to pursue open discussions, promoting a new perspective and perhaps more accurate information.

Take this True/False Self-discovery Quiz:

Statements:	Circle One:
1. You can always tell a 'stud'or 'hot babe' when you see one, meaning you know they are good in the sack.	True or False?
2. Meaningful communication is the key to good sex.	True or False?

3. A woman's orgasm is very different from a man's.	True or False?
4. Roughly 90% of a vagina's nerve endings are in the top third of that region.	True or False?
5. A woman's vagina can accommodate any penis.	True or False?
6. Having periodic mechanical sex means you no longer love your mate.	True or False?
7. Every lover should know how to be "romantic." It's a natural instinct.	True or False?
8. Foreplay is important for a woman's satisfaction.	True or False?
9. Good sex is 90% mental.	True or False?
10. Penis size contributes to enhanced pleasure.	True or False?

CHECK YOUR ANSWERS:

<u>By sight only, knowing if someone is good in the sack.</u>

#1. FALSE. You can't always tell who hot and who's not. There are no absolutes about love, sex, and pleasure. We've all heard the cliche, "You can't judge a book by its cover." Well, there's lots of truth to this. Clearly, if you notice an attractive person who is genuinely confident and comfortable in their skin, it's more likely that he is enthusiastic in bed. Conversely, though, a gorgeous person can be frigid while many plain-looking men and women are the most passionate in bed.

A local psychologist in the Phoenix area—Dr. Bob Bohanske—once told me some incredible stories about his clients (without breaking confidentiality). A few were internationally-known models (including one Miss Universe) who had difficulty sustaining a relationship for any length of time, much less enjoy sex. She described herself as a cold fish and wanted help to break the pattern of unsatisfying sex. For all of her physical beauty, this model didn't feel sexy at all.

In this case, the model primarily received attention based solely on her looks. When others handled her as an object, she learned to treat herself as one. By objectifying herself, she never learned to express her more real vulnerable side. A former Miss Universe never felt loved; she felt esteemed like a piece of art. It's an oxymoron that a world-renowned beauty found it difficult to be loving or receive love. Sex became an obligatory chore because of her status, never an expression of caring or affection. She felt lifeless during the act. She could not pretend to be an eager participant anymore, so she finally reached out for help.

It may be easier for a modest-looking woman to embrace intimacy, knowing her partner is not mainly interested in her appearance. Every woman wants to feel valued and appreciated in spite of her physical beauty. This confidence and respect must begin with the woman embracing her femininity and loving herself completely. She has the freedom to feel sexy from the inside out.

Meaningful communication is the key to good sex.

#2. TRUE. Whether with words or gestures, we connect to others. Touch is one of the most profound ways to communicate. Remember it's the total package that benefits us: words, voice tone, and body language. Studies show that words account for roughly seven to ten percent of our message. During sex, a few sweet nothings add spice. Your tone of voice accounts for about 33% of the message.

Again, a grunt, groan, and natural sounds work here. Over the phone, your voice tone counts for about 70% of the meaning. Body language for the remaining 57%, which includes gesturing. Perhaps it's as high as up to 99% during sex! Since most of us use a combination of these, I offer some exercises in week seven to expand your horizons in this area. Stay tuned!

A woman's orgasm is very different from a man's.

#3. SPLIT DECISION. 50% TRUE, 50% FALSE. This similar orgasm business is a matter of interpretation. Viva la difference! Many aspects of an orgasm are the same for men and women; other aspects are quite different.

Only by anecdotal means can it be shown that the physical sensations feel the same. Perhaps we could ask a transgender person this question.

Definition: An orgasm is an automatic reflex that results in contractions lasting .08 of a second each in both males and females. The amount of fluid expelled is roughly the same. The process of friction, build up, and release is physiologically similar.

A woman's orgasm varies more dramatically in regards to length, type, and frequency. Every man is unable to have multiple orgasms the way a woman can. Any woman with a clitoris can develop a capacity for multiple orgasms. A woman can have dozens in a single session. Men just can't match those numbers.

<u>Roughly 90% of a vagina's nerve endings are
in the top third of that region.</u>

#4. TRUE. Studies by both Johnson & Johnson the Kinsey report shows that approximately 90% of a vagina's nerve endings are located in the top third of the vaginal canal. This is good news. The length of a penis is not as necessary for pleasure as people think. Rather, it's the motion of the ocean that counts.

<u>A woman's vagina can accommodate any penis.</u>

#5. TRUE. Generally speaking, a vagina can accommodate any penis. A woman's vagina is very elastic. And unless there is a medical condition (e.g. stenosis) that prohibits sex, a woman can accept a very large penis.

<u>Having periodic mechanical sex means you no longer love your mate.</u>

#6. FALSE. Mechanical sex is a part of life. Mature love recognizes that human moods, energy levels, limits and stress play a role. Have you ever asked your partner, "Are you in the mood tonight? Are we having fun yet? Are you ready to come?" The sex may be pleasant enough, but the timing isn't the best. Consequently, what is usually passionate becomes merely satisfactory. Tell your partner, "Well, I could use a break, but you go ahead and come." Write it off and get on with your life. Don't dwell on an imperfect act. So it wasn't ideal timing. Whatever. Any negative energy only expands. Be mature. Focus on another task or activity right away. Besides, the next time you have sex, it might be the best.

<u>Every lover should know how to be romantic. It's a natural instinct.</u>

#7. FALSE. Being romantic is not a natural instinct. It's a learned behavior. Most men never realize why a candlelight dinner and a pleasant conversation causes their mate to desire them more than usual. For women, it's about the ambiance. A man typically wakes up horny. He only looks at his scantily-clothed wife lying next to him, and he's ready. He may proceed to have his way with her if given the green light. When his wife is equally ready, it's great. Sometimes animal-like. But, hey, nothing is wrong with that! Many times, though, it's not a magical experience. Accept that and be grateful for the loving connection.

Most lovers could learn a few tricks from the 1988 movie, Bull Durham, by watching Crash Davis interact with the woman he loves. He's sweet, yet manly. Perceptive. Poetic. Strong. Unique. Ladies could take lessons from Annie Savoy's sensual independence in this movie, too.

<u>Foreplay is important for a woman's satisfaction.</u>

#8. TRUE. Foreplay is apparently more crucial for women than most men. However, this is not always the case. It depends on which man and which woman. Some women warm up quickly. The first kiss signals that they want sex. Others have told me it takes them thirty to forty-five minutes to get in the mood even though they love their husband. Compromise is a good thing. Realistically, a man can't be expected to take that long every love-making session just to get his wife ready.

The pressure would be too overwhelming, and he would not want to initiate sex as often if foreplay becomes a long chore. A woman could compromise by warming herself up earlier or using a sensation-improving lubrication. Some men, especially as they age, cannot be rushed. They need a little extra time to get an erection. So, enjoy the extra snuggle time. Feel the love. Feel the joy.

<u>Good sex is mostly mental.</u>

#9. TRUE. Good sex is 90% mental. Knowing the so-called proper technique does not mean the act will always go well. Of course, I've talked to many men and women who claim never to have experienced bad sex. The more honest ones, though, will admit to not enjoying the act because of emotional or mental reasons. Perhaps guilt of betraying a spouse overshadows the enjoyment, or the partner does not respond the way he/she anticipated. Consequently, sex becomes emotionless and without joy.

<u>Penis size matters.</u>

#10. TRUE & FALSE. This is not a trick question, but rather it's a matter of preference. The size of a man's penis is not usually an issue for pleasing a woman. However, some women prefer a larger-than-average size. A sizable penis is not physiologically necessary for an orgasm. For some women who want the 'full feeling,' a long penis is important because the right mental mindset is critical for heightened sexual pleasure. They simply prefer the fullness for psychological reasons.

In my book, *How to Have Multiple Orgasms* (Avon Books), I wrote:

"The Worth is in the Girth."

I discussed the importance of circumference because friction on the clitoris is more likely with a hefty penis. And that, my friend, is the source of intense pleasure.

Do Your Beliefs, Values, and Experiences Play a Role in Your Sex Life Today?

Take the time now to think back to the first time you heard about, visualized, or had sexual intercourse. Relax, clear your mind, focus, close your eyes, uncross your legs and arms. Whatever works for you. Remember, this is a tool for self-discovery and you may learn something new about your partner.

1. How did you learn about sexual intercourse? How old were you? Did your first sexual experience match up to your expectations? Why or why not?

His: _____

_____

_____

_____

_____

_____

Hers: _____

_____

_____

_____

_____

_____

2. How did you learn about oral sex? Was your relationship with your first lover a close one? How did the experience make you feel when you first received/performed oral sex? What do you think about it now?

His: _____

_____

_____

_____

_____

_____

Hers: _____

_____

_____

_____

_____

3. Has sex improved for you over time? Why or why not?

His: _____

_____

_____

_____

_____

_____

Hers: _____

_____

_____

_____

_____

4. What do you like most about sex? How big a role does romantic love play for enjoying sex? There's no right or wrong answer. Express your opinion. Talk.

His: _____

_____

_____

_____

_____

Hers: _____

_____

_____

_____

_____

Erotic Discovery Exercise

Now is a good time for you to try a couple of new activities because you've shared some intimate details about yourselves. This is a great chance to reinforce some of the things you've learned so far. Devote the next fifteen to thirty minutes to positively reinforce your boyfriend or girlfriend. This is a fun activity that can be added to your bedroom repertoire.

Follow These Simple Steps:

A. Start with a set period, say ten minutes, to begin.
B. Designate a <u>Giver</u> and a <u>Receiver</u>.
C. Choose a particular sexual activity.
D. The <u>Receiver</u> offers verbal feedback (on a scale from 1-100).
E. The <u>Giver</u> makes an effort to diversify the activities.

<u>Suggested Activities:</u>

bun-biting	ear-licking
breast-fondling	foot-rubbing
toe-sucking	back-scratching
tummy-patting	clitoris-tonguing
neck-kissing	scalp massaging
butt-squeezing	nipple-twisting

Use these as a springboard. Let your imagination run wild. For instance, the <u>Giver</u> may ask, "Do you like X or Y better when I rub this? Do you like it slower or faster? Deep or moderate pressure? Do you like it when I touch you 'here' at the same time?"

Did you learn one new thing about your partner? Great!

Trade places. Be specific in your feedback so your partner is clear about what you like and what you don't like. For instance, "It feels good when you nibble and lick me slow first because my body adjusts better to your speed and intensity." Also, you need to be 100% truthful with your lover, "Oh, that tickles me instead of excites me."

This Erotic Discovery Exercise is good for the body and the soul!

Thanks for your honesty!
Week Four Challenge:
Exploring Beliefs and Core Values

CHAPTER 5

WEEK FIVE CHALLENGE: DISPELLING MYTHS AND MISCONCEPTIONS

#1: The Clitoral-Vaginal Myth:

First, let's get technical for a minute.

What are the nuts and bolts of an orgasm? An orgasm is an automatic reflex that happens once the body, particularly the clitoris, has been stimulated adequately and is expressed by contractions. For a woman, the shaft and glans of the clitoris become swollen with blood and expand about thirty times its un-aroused size. This can be likened to the tip of a man's penis. The rest of the underlying structure of a woman rests internally, of course, but it's roughly the same size as the genitalia of a male. In fact, the total amount of blood vessel engorgement during arousal can equal or exceed that of a penis.

For a female, it's incorrect to say that you had a vaginal orgasm. Clinical research shows that there is no orgasm without tactile friction applied directly or indirectly to the clitoris. So, technically, it is incorrect to say 'vaginal orgasm.' This term is simply an imperfect anatomical way of explaining the difference. It's important to note that the placement of a woman's clitoris plays a role in her ability to have an orgasm successfully.

After surveying roughly one hundred women in the San Francisco Bay area, 15% admitted they were able to have multiple orgasms through intercourse. However, 67% were unable to have multiple orgasms while the remaining 18% were either confused or were unsure if they had ever experienced one. The respondents were between the ages of twenty and fifty-five from a variety of economic and ethnic backgrounds. You can determine what category you fall into based on these statistics. If you have found it difficult to have an orgasm, please know that many women are in the same boat.

Yes, of course, most people are only referring to the method of stimulation when they say 'vaginal orgasm.' Every orgasm reflex has a motor and sensory component. The physical expression or motor component is expressed by contractions in and around the vagina. The sensory component is the location of the trigger.

The types of stimulation are as varied as your imagination:

1) **Manually-stimulated** orgasms have many variations including the use of a finger, hand, vibrator, or other sex toys. There's relief of sexual tension no matter what causes the arousal. During masturbation, orgasms feel as intense as a woman can handle. Because of the little emotional impact, though, sometimes women feel there is little depth to them, no guts so to speak. Mainly just a physical release. Many women find manually-stimulated orgasms more intense than penetration ones.

2) **Orally-stimulated** orgasms can feel smooth, soft and sometimes powerful or intense depending on the particular technique. The genital area feels a warmth and pressure which cannot be matched by any other means of stimulation. Cunnilingus—oral sex performed on female genitalia—can feel marvelously primitive and basic, intimate in a special way. It is fairly common for women to have a series of orgasms during cunnilingus.

3) **Penetration orgasms** often elicit a more diffused, softer, gentler

sensation. It is possible to discover the same excitement of intense orgasms through penetration, masturbation, and oral sex. A woman can learn to experience an orgasm within seconds after penetration, especially after an excellent foreplay session.

You feel building up of tension that starts in a core spot inside your vagina, which then extends outward like the ripples in a pond. Suddenly, it's like the entire dam breaks, and the pressure is relieved. That's what happens as the blood surrounding the vaginal wall is built up and then released. Yes, the same level of intensity can be achieved with all methods, once you've discovered your capacity for having orgasms.

Let's talk about how an orgasm feels. See if this rings true for you. In the well-known book, *The Hite Report*, women describe an orgasm like this:

- refreshing, exciting, energizing
- pulsating, engulfing, alive
- opening feeling in the vagina
- sweaty hotness, tingling
- exploding pleasure, fulfilling
- an intense pulling sensation
- being on the edge of an earthquake

However you describe it, it's a positively glorious feeling. Agreed? If you haven't experienced one yet, read on.

How Are Orgasms Achieved?

Men and women have orgasms via four basic sources of stimulation:

- By manual manipulation
- By oral stimulation
- By vaginal intercourse
- By anal intercourse

Make no mistake, a woman's clitoris has to be stimulated for an orgasm to occur while a man's external organ is, of course, a different story. In spite of the fact that all orgasms are physiologically identical, don't they feel differently to you? I encourage you and your partner to use terms you both agree on so you can communicate more directly.

Alert your spouse to the type of stimulation you want or need at a particular time. It's fun to make up your wording for what you want.

#2-Misconceptions about Types of Orgasms

Some experts categorize orgasms into four basic types:

I.   Single
II. Sequential
III. Multiple
IV. Peritoneal

<u>Single</u> means one orgasm. Simple.

<u>Multiple</u> refers to more than one orgasm during a lovemaking session, but with a definite rest period in between. So it's like a series of single orgasms with many seconds or several minutes breaking up the tension after each one, with time to build up to the next. Typically these exhibit varying degrees of intensity.

<u>Sequential</u> is more unique. It's like a stream of orgasms, one right after another. With no break in between. Individually, these are less intense. The entire experience, however, is emotionally fulfilling as well as physically draining. But it's wonderfully relaxing. You'll feel like a wet wash rag when finished.

<u>Peritoneal</u> involves the peritoneum, a membrane which lines the abdominal cavity. This type is very explosive. It could be considered a variation of the single. For both men and women, the peritoneal orgasm gives deep ecstatic pleasure. If you're striving for a different sensation, try stimulating the peritoneum, area between the anus and the vagina. Your partner's hand can gently rub the membrane lining on the outside while his penis aims for

internal stimulation. It requires the deepest penetration possible, typically with the woman on top, or if preferred, in a sitting position.

The peritoneal orgasm is considered by some to be the most elusive orgasm of all. Any indirect frictional tension around the clitoral shaft caused by the motion of the penis works. It's easier to have this type when you're not striving for it. But you know it by its intensity when you find it. Perhaps you already have this type, but you've never attached a name to it. They are very intense and happen only once. That's why many consider it a single explosive one.

Words fall short of the ecstatic experience. Your entire body will become electrified, shaking and trembling, stiffening uncontrollably for what seems like a long time. Orgasms last only a few seconds up to about thirty seconds in actuality. As with most intense orgasms, time stands still, suspended, turning into a dreamlike eternity.

Your body may feel as if it has enveloped the universe. You may be lightheaded, boarding on a fainting spell, in a limitless dimension of time and space. You may be more content, more willing to return to the realities of the day, more aware of being a purposeful individual. You'll feel magical and majestic.

A lifetime of better sex is worth a few moments of clumsiness. Right? As a couple, how do you talk about sex? Some use proper terms while most partners prefer slang. Don't you want to learn what turns on your spouse? Okay, then, be brave. What words are a turn-on? Turn-offs? Establish boundaries.

You can move your lover's hand directly to where you want it, but sometimes that feels clumsy or awkward. When gentle and smooth, it works like a charm.

In this next exercise, decide what words and phrases easily alert your lover to what you want during sex. Both of you take a separate sheet of paper and write down what words you'd prefer to use for a variety of sex acts. How do you want to be stimulated right now? For example, "I want a blow job.

Will you go down on me? I want oral sex." To avoid miscommunication in the bedroom, you need to good on the same page ahead of time.

If you can't talk about sex, maybe you can discover the reasons behind your shyness. Perhaps it's upbringing, religious background or inexperience that leads to an inability to vocalize your wants and needs. Some married partners haven't had these sorts of discussions even after decades of marriage. Chapter six helps you overcome some of these barriers.

Do you make specific requests or do you just go along for the ride? Involved lovers make better connections. Does everything just flow naturally? Don't be shy to make your needs known at a particular time, something which turns you on like, "Go down on me so I'll be ready for you." Saliva is one of the quickest methods for lubrication. It's easy and readily available.

Let each person write down their favorite word choices below or if they'd prefer something different. Some prefer when their partner gets nasty or uses foul language while others don't care for that at all. Find out.

Stimulation Type:	Her choice:	His choice:
Manually		
Orally		
Vaginal Penetration		
Anal Penetration		

If it's so natural, though, why do some women take so long to have an orgasm? Others never get there. Men admit to how frustrating it is when they know their wife is aroused, but she seldom seems to climax. "Is she preventing an orgasm or am I to blame?"

Stopping an orgasm is like stopping your sneeze. It's possible, and in fact, many women succeed in sabotaging their orgasms. Can you stop a sneeze?

Sure, sometimes. We've all attempted to stifle one in public. Likewise, you can curtail your orgasm. Let's look at ways women, and a few men, unintentionally undermine their pleasure:

- Uptight about sex in general
- Too much objectivity (in their head)
- Lack of emotional involvement
- Self-conscious about how they look
- Embarrassed about how they sound
- Intoxicated by alcohol/drugs
- Anxious personality type
- Playing a spectator role
- Worried about getting pregnant
- Overly stressed out
- Feelings of guilt
- Rx medications that interfere with libido

For some people, it's best to refocus attention on their partner. Others turn inward and attend to the present moment and what they need to do to increase physical sensations. Trying too hard can hinder your plans and sabotage your pleasure. Practice relaxation techniques on a regular basis for better results.

#3: Are Synchronized Orgasms the Ultimate Experience?

In my opinion, simultaneous orgasms are overrated.

Don't get me wrong; they can be fantastic. It can be a very moving experience—literally and emotionally—when it happens. Far too often, couples strive so hard for a synchronized orgasm that they miss the experience of expressing love and affection. Besides, it's the woman who is let down periodically because of premature ejaculation. At least it's early from her perspective.

Many young men can't control their bodies well enough to time their orgasm; their pleasure supersedes their partners. Give a young guy a break, ladies. Fortunately, a man in his prime has recuperative powers that are extraordinary. So the second (or third) time around, his orgasm builds up much slower, allowing his lover to experience her climax. Men can learn to pace themselves.

A caring man enjoys giving his partner pleasure first because then he feels better about ejaculating when he wants. If the woman happens to come again during his orgasm, fine. If not, it's no big deal because she is already satisfied. I think the movies (and porn) have portrayed simultaneous climaxes as the ultimate experience.

New or inexperienced lovers, in particular, are unprepared for the reality of accomplishing this feat. Practically speaking, focusing on a timed activity can spoil the moment. Male egos are fragile. Think of the pressure a man is under to hold back physically. If he's young, there can always be another round. Some people, especially at a certain age, aren't able to get hard again the same night.

One man I interviewed told me that the most devastating words he can hear during sex are, "Don't come yet." It hurts his ego because he realizes that he hasn't satisfied her yet. Again, it's like a spectacle instead of a loving and caring exchange of genuine affection.

Movies portray the both-at-the-same-time orgasm as the ideal sexual experience. In the real world, however, here is what the dialogue might sound like between a couple trying to accomplish the so-called perfect sex act:

> Jack: I'm almost there.
> Jill: Hurry up.
> Jill: I'm trying.
> Jack: Oh, please, honey.
> Jill: Slow down.
> Jack: I can't wait any longer.
> Jill: Hold back.
> Jack: Okay, okay.

Jill: I'm not ready yet.
Jack: I'm coming, baby, I'm coming.
Jill: No, no, no.
Jack: Aaaaaaaaaaaaaaaaaaaah!
Jill: Dammit Jack!

A woman might prefer to climax with her partner, but often it doesn't work that way. She may become agitated or feel desperate to have her partner wait. If you focus too much on a perfectly-timing simultaneous orgasm, sex becomes a circus. Jack and Jill participated in a carnival act, like a plate-spinning entertainer in Vegas. If one plate stops spinning, they all fall, just like Jack and Jill do, and frustration ensues.

In a mature relationship, the woman ought to signal the man that she is sexually spent or has had enough and that it is the man's turn now. Then everybody's happy. This routine becomes second nature when practiced on a regular basis. Of course, sex shouldn't be put on a replay loop either.

The male also needs to communicate his dilemma. Like a catch-22, he may feel like he can't win. What is a man to do if he's earnestly tried to please his partner for a long time (twenty to thirty minutes) while his partner still has not climaxed? The couple can, at this point, agree that he ejaculates first.

An agreement could be discussed ahead of time. Select a phrase such as, "Your turn next, honey," when your partner realizes his hard-on won't last or due to early ejaculation challenges. As promised, your mate then should take care of your needs orally or otherwise after a recuperative period.

Men's bodies produce chemicals that cause them to be sleepy after climaxing. So, ladies, let them nap. You may want one, too. By the way, anyone can learn ways to control bodily functions. All it takes is desire, practice, and maturity.

Timing your orgasms may be a good a topic for discussion at some point in your relationship. Jot down any feelings, impressions, and ideas you each have regarding simultaneous orgasms. This is a good time to be honest.

Your Thoughts on Simultaneous Orgasms:

His: _____

_____

_____

_____

_____

_____

Hers: _____

_____

_____

_____

_____

#4-Myths Surrounding Self-Pleasure

Masturbation is a normal part of life. And a healthy outlet, too. A clear majority of men and women have masturbated at some time in their lives. Some studies believe that it's as high as 90% of the population. For some people, self-pleasure reaches its height during adolescence. For others, it becomes a habit during periods of loneliness, stress, separation, or loss of a loved one in adulthood. Masturbation is a healthy routine to achieve a physical release when needed. Our mental health, in part, rests on the physical release of sexual tension.

In all fairness to men, women should know their bodies well enough to give themselves an orgasm. A man cannot read a woman's mind. Yes, trial and error usually work. But what negative psychological pattern is occurring in the meantime? Try different tools, vibrators, techniques to figure out what works best for you. Again, your physical needs vary from one day to the next.

The biggest takeaway from this chapter is about personal responsibility. If a woman can't climax by herself, how does she expect a man to know how to please her? The following statement applies to both genders:

If you think about it, we use electrical devices to help us enhance the quality of our lives. On any given day, we may use a toaster, an electric shaver, a flashlight, a microwave or a hair dryer. So why is a vibrator considered unnatural or a crutch? Is it any different than an alarm clock to get us up in the morning? Think of a vibrator as a tool like any other device used for efficiency and convenience.

Jot Down Your Thoughts &Feelings:

His: _____

_____

_____

_____

_____

_____

Hers: _____

_____

_____

_____

_____

_____

Be true to yourself and not influenced by what the other writes or thinks.

By being your authentic self, you'll truly grow during this seven-week challenge and improve your relationship.

Is a Vibrator Superficial or Spectacular?

Both genders deserve to have a physical release without the constraints and demands of having a partner to fulfill their needs. What's perfect about a vibrator is that you can vary the speed by a push of a button. You can also change the pitch, angle, and pressure for a unique set of sensations.

Sometimes after being given an electric vibrator, even as a gag gift, women soon discover it's no joke. Some vibrators have attachments so you can try different styles. There's a broad range of dildo types you can find at any adult shop. After a sexual release, aren't you able to think more clearly?

The Many Advantages of Self-pleasure:

- Simple
- Available
- Safe
- Relaxing
- Effective
- Legal
- Pregnant-proof
- Burns calories

Self-pleasuring also: adds variety, enriches fantasy life, supports mental health, leads to self-discovery, teaches us how to love yourself, improves mental clarity, and requires no emotional attachment. Sometimes, it's just what the doctor ordered.

Be aware of your breathing. Deep abdominal breathing relaxes your body best. Observe how your breathing rhythm quickens before climaxing. The more awareness you have of your body, the more control you gain when you're with a partner. Once you know the signs and how to open up your meridians—energy channels throughout your body—a woman will be able to climax much more easily with a man.

While purposely building up to an intense orgasm, you can bring your body to near-climax several times. With more pressure directly on the clitoris, it's time for business. Like a roller coaster, you can achieve a magically-suspended sensation with less weight and then move slower, like trudging up a large hill on a ride. Then your body stiffens for a long, intense orgasm.

Experiment with the different types of stimulation. With practice, you may be able to go for ten to twenty minutes or more of continuous pleasure before stopping. You'll be amazed at your capacity once you become comfortable with your body.

Most of the research suggests that men and women who choose to masturbate regularly are more likely to be easily aroused and multi-orgasmic. They say it enhances their desire and pleasure with a partner. Some admit that while it feels good physically, masturbation leaves them feeling empty.

It's a good reminder that a physical release assists with a healthy mental state. Remember, when you choose to self-pleasure, you wire your brain for intensified pleasure with your partner the next time you engage in sex.

What Range of Emotions Do You Feel?

Does the subject of self-pleasuring create positive or negative feelings for you? Many people accept it as a part of life, especially during periods of separation or stress. Others feel foolish, guilty, lonely, self-conscious or ashamed. Substitute a more reasonable statement for the non-rational tapes that play in your head: "I have the right to have a physical release if I need one."

Do you masturbate? Why or why not? How do you feel when you masturbate? Why do you think you feel this way? Background? Experiences? Religion? Parents? Peer Pressure? Even if you don't know why you feel the way you do, write down what comes to mind about self-pleasuring.

Jot Down Your Thoughts & Impressions:

His: _____

_____

_____

_____

_____

_____

Hers: _____

_____

_____

_____

_____

Of course, there's sense of connection and a depth of emotion attached when an orgasm is shared. But with a good imagination, you can feel a variety of emotions when you're alone as well. Think about it. Why is an orgasm more valuable if you're with your partner? Sex with your mate may provide an emotional connection, but that may not be your goal at a particular moment.

It makes no sense to deprive yourself of something so natural. Even babies and toddlers investigate their genitalia. It's part of exploring their environment. In trying to help both genders enjoy a fuller taste of passion and pleasurable sensations, it's critical that each person explores his or her body.

Understanding your body's potential for pleasure teaches you to be receptive to your partner's real passion. This knowledge promotes loving and spirited sex.

Strictly speaking on a physical level, it provides many health benefits. Do you know how many calories are burned during an orgasm? Studies show that you can burn between sixty and one hundred calories when having an orgasm (that includes the ramp-up). A half hour of sex burns roughly 144 to 207 calories. So enjoy!

For more information regarding orgasms, check out Mikaya Heart's book, *The Ultimate Guide to Orgasm for Women: How to Become Orgasmic for a Lifetime.* She writes:

> "Forget that cup of coffee! An orgasm may be all you need when you want a little charge in the morning. Orgasm realigns the energy in the body and removes blocks to the natural energy flow, making us feel more alive and present.
>
> Having regular orgasms may be a very good remedy for people who are in chronic pain. Experiments have shown that when a woman is in an orgasmic state, she doesn't even feel pain that might otherwise send her through the roof.
>
> When we reach orgasm with a partner, we connect to them on a deeper level. It's a way of assessing a reality that is much greater than our daily grind."

Of course it's important to share the deep and profound love that is shared via an orgasm with your partner. Still, it's marvelous thing when you climax by yourself. In fact, the health benefits alone are worth it!

Whether or not there's a partner in your life, you shouldn't automatically stop masturbating. There will still be periods of stress, loneliness, or separation even in a good partnership.

Self-pleasure is a normal and healthy outlet for both genders. When practiced regularly, you will:

1. Think clearly.
2. Be more creative.
3. Lower blood pressure.
4. Be more relaxed.
5. Enjoy better blood flow.
6. Remove energy blocks.
7. Be in less pain.
8. Savor activities longer.
9. Connect easily with your partner.

Somewhat oddly, both genders I interviewed said they were offended when they caught their spouse masturbating, unfairly blasting them for this perfectly natural self-indulgent deed. Surely, each has a right to self-satisfaction. Isn't it twisted logic to assume you are the only person who should activate your lover's orgasm? Your partner has human needs and the right to masturbate for physical release when needed.

Some faulted themselves for not measuring up to the challenge of adequately taking care of their spouse's needs; others blamed their mate for not being honest with them about their actual needs. Remember, though, everyone has the right to privacy and the right to self-pleasure.

A majority have some positive emotions related to giving themselves pleasure. They enjoy the experience physically without the demands, time commitment, and social interaction involved. Some get turned on by watching their partner masturbate. Masturbation is a matter of choice.

The reality of modern society is that many people go without a sex partner for long periods in their lives due to divorce, separation, widowhood, or by choice. As you can see, there's a broad range of emotional responses to the subject. Choose what's best in the long run, but keep an open mind.

You deserve to treat yourself to an orgasm whenever you want one. Let your body and heart be your guide!

#5: Misconceptions about Sex & Menses

Some women have declared that they never have sex during their period. That means they avoid sex for three to five days every month? Maybe a few more. Other females say, "That's crazy talk." Embrace our heterogeneity of perspectives and celebrate our diverse opinions.

Granted, some women have severe premenstrual cramping, and I'm not saying you shouldn't take a break. Rest. Recuperate. It's nature's way of telling women to slow down and be still.

This topic came up so many times in my seminars that I feel it's important to address the issue. The discussion with revealed a few possibilities for why women don't engage in sex at this time of the month:

1. Sex wasn't all that important for them, so giving it up a small percentage of the time isn't a big deal.
2. Their physical symptoms are so severe or painful that they really don't enjoy doing much of anything at that time of the month;
3. They thought is was dirty, unnatural, or gross.
4. Beliefs begin at a young age. One mother told her daughter never to have sex during menses; her daughter accepted this as fact so she didn't try until she was nearly thirty-five. She loved it.

There is no physical reason to avoid intercourse during menses. Oral sex may be delayed, but that too depends on each couple. Sex during your period can be beautiful. The body is warm.

There's little risk of becoming pregnant. Admittedly, if you practice birth control, you will reduce the chances of having a baby and the stress that comes with starting a family. The sensations are incredible.

In fact, numerous women report that sex during menses is their favorite time. Their hormones are heightened, and their body responds easily to most any stimulation.

Be open and try it a few times. You might like it.

#6: Sex & Parenthood Misconceptions

Yes, there is sex after parenthood. Unfortunately, it sometimes has to be planned in advance. Or wait until after the baby or kids are asleep. Perhaps wait until after your nap. It's tougher than when you lived together without children. That's a given. Since sex is the glue that keeps couples together, though, it's important to make the time for each other, even if it is less often.

Mature men are patient for a while after delivery. Don't expect your wife to want sex a few days after giving birth, especially if it's a natural delivery and a nine-pound baby came through her vaginal canal. It's an exhausting business, guys. Heck, many doctors recommend waiting three to six weeks for a full recovery. Every new mother is different. Six weeks is a stretch, but there are other ways to get sexual tension relieved besides penetration. Try to think of it as a time to explore the various sensations through the erotic discovery exercises posted in week four.

Having sex while your child is a baby or a toddler is usually a challenge. If there are other children in the household, it gets even tougher because of the increased family demands on both partners.

Parents, especially new mothers, are exhausted much of the time. It's difficult to schedule times to be alone. Unpredictable events happen. Just when you've decided to go on a sweet romantic home date, one of your dear children comes down with the measles or worse.

A couple must make attempts at keeping their romantic life alive. The best gift you can give your children is for them to see how strong your relationship is. Intimacy is enhanced if your sex life is passionate and regular.

Wait until your baby or toddler is asleep and then enjoy sex or cuddle if that's all the energy you have left. Make the most of your secluded moments. Inform older children that parents need quality time with each other. Signal your need for privacy by locking your bedroom and by hanging a tie or special sign around the doorknob to prevent interruptions.

Spoiled children who believe they are the center of the universe become bigger problems (nearly unsolvable) when they are teenagers. So, remind your precious toddler that it is a fact of life that they are part of a family unit. The parents rule the roost, not the other way around. Every member of the family takes a turn in getting attention at different times. It's natural.

Don't we all know a few adults who never grew out of the belief that they are the center of the universe? These people sometimes find it difficult to maintain genuine friendships and romantic relationships. So, there's the rub.

Create Time For Conscious Coupling

Try to get out for an evening, a day, or a weekend trip at least once a month when your children are still young. A relative or sitter helps them adjust to a broader world that awaits them and helps prepare them for the different personality styles of teachers and others down the road. Kids are sponges and they pick up more than we give them credit for sometimes.

Leaving your children with someone who has a different parenting style is not necessarily a bad thing. Unless there is a behavioral goal you're working where consistency is key, a parent need not worry about a sitter running the household differently for a short time. Children learn how to adapt to a variety of personalities, which will serve them later in life.

Like the old analogy goes: a two-legged table is unstable, but three or more legs keep it balanced and secure. A threesome, mother-mother-child, mother-father-child, or father-father figure-child, is a stronger unit as long as the twosome provides a solid base. The same holds true for a larger family.

One of the greatest gifts you can give your children is for them to grow up observing devoted and loving parents on a day-to-day basis. Equally important is for them to see how you resolve your differences in a mature way. A sexual relationship is a big part of what holds a couple together.

Keep the fires stoked by using the communication techniques and erotic exercises mentioned in this workbook or by whatever methods work best for you as a couple. If you're a parent, some of the best sex of your life may happen after your children become teenagers who gladly give you as much privacy as you want.

Take it one day at a time. It's a team effort to raise your children while putting your marriage or relationship first. In this way, you are serving your kids well. Yes, there are distinct times when parents must put a child's needs first; but you must maintain a balance, or your relationship will sour.

Look to each for love and affection. Over the years, many men have revealed that they strayed from their marriage because they felt like they were at the bottom of the family totem pole. The children got 100% of the attention. These men wanted to feel loved, valued, and appreciated.

This holds true for women as well. Do your best to keep each other at the top of the totem pole. Your children will turn out to be more independent youngsters and adults in the long run. They learn to pattern their relationship around this idea that it's important to keep the fires stoked.

#7: Sex & Aging Misconceptions

For the young and vintage couples alike, I have great news! There's a saying about getting older and sex and it goes like this:

The Older the Violin, the Sweeter the Music!

When I was a teenager, I wondered if my parents still had sex. My mom was forty-three, and my dad was fifty years old. Weren't they over the hill? Gosh, how naive I was back then! Most of my middle-aged friends still feel and act young. They have sex on a regular basis, some even more than they did in their twenties or thirties. In many cases, these couples the have more leisure time on their hands and more money to spend doing activities they enjoy together.

A fun fact: in Victorian times, many women experienced their first orgasm after age forty because their spouses were no longer in a big hurry to climax. This is a common change for men as they get older, which provides their partner a better chance to enjoy sex. Some wives were begging for more time in the bedroom. What a stunner for these men! I wonder if any Victorian woman turned to her husband, "So this is what I've been missing all these years!" The information and clinical knowledge were not available in the 1800's. Besides, the subject of sex was not discussed openly in polite society.

To be sure, I've met couples in their 40's, 50's, and 60's that enjoy sex frequently. Some fifty-somethings have sex nearly every day. Now that the kids are grown, they have more time and energy. Work is not as stressful as it used to be. And they are mature enough to explore new activities in the bedroom.

Free Activities For Couples:

As usual, you have a choice to reinforce your partner the way you want, even if you choose to do nothing—because that in and of itself is a selection.

1. Go to a park, if you live in the city, or pick a spot outdoors. Bring a blanket and a little picnic snack and watch a sunset. Either quietly (or not), absorb the mystery of the universe. Out of the billions of people on the planet, recognize that you chose to share this moment with each other.

2. How about washing your partner's hair in a bathtub or shower? Remember to suds up other regions, too. Continue to splash and indulge. Have fun, but proceed safely.

3. Write a simple poem to your significant other.

If you think you are not creative, then you have a couple of choices: Pick from something online. Select a topic (Love, Intimacy, Romance, Spooning), and then each writes down the first ten words that come to mind. Now reverse the order of those ten words and read your new creative poem out loud. You'll be surprised how poetic you can be.

Read with feeling. Come on; you can do better than that. Try writing some poetry for other occasions. Use this inventive method and expand each word into a sentence or two. Becoming a poet is easier than you think.

Well done! You've succeeded in completing
Week Five Challenge:
Dispelling Myths and Misconceptions

CHAPTER 6

WEEK SIX CHALLENGE: STRENGTHENING CROSS-GENDER COMMUNICATION

As we talked about in week two, you are either moving closer to or away from intimacy at any given time. You make a choice every day. In fact, moment by moment you choose to be lovable, faithful, considerate, genuine, fun, kind, supportive, humorous, joyful, patient, gentle, self-controlled.

Take This Communication-Enhancing Discovery Quiz:

- How many times per week do you share something important?
- What does high-quality communication mean to you?
- On a scale from 1-10, how well do you express yourself?
- Does your level of communication match your partner's level?
- Do you feel that he/she honestly listens to you?
- Are you satisfied with your current level of talking?
- Do you know what excites your partner in bed?
- Can you depend on the other person at critical times in your life?

Jot down Answers, Ideas, & Impressions

His: _____

_____

_____

_____

_____

_____

Hers: _____

_____

_____

_____

_____

A Focused-Language, Communication Activity (F-L-C-A):

Take turns. Like you did during week two, follow the same rules during the Focused-Listening, Intimacy Exchange (F-L-I-E) exercise. Flip a coin to see who goes first. Let's say the Partner A begins and asks the questions:

1. On a scale from one to ten, where do you see our communication level now?
2. Where would you like it to be (on the same scale)?
3. What can I do to move us from a #_____to a #_____?

Remember to follow these rules. They're the same as before.

The questioner may not talk.**
You questioner may not argue.
You questioner may not criticize.
You questioner may not interrupt.
You questioner may not give excuses.

**A clarification question is fine, such as "Can you give me an example?"

Note: Keep in mind that this exercise is to learn what makes your lover tick. It's like a gentle, mental reminder to both parties that you can't always read your partner's mind.

Let your partner's answers sink in. Recognize there's at least a hint of truth behind the answers. Tweak your behavior for more peace and harmony in your relationship. It's a two-way street.

Your job is to listen, pay attention, and soak it up simply.

The Do's & Don'ts of Communication
In the Bedroom

Reserve your bedroom for sleeping, reading, relaxing or lovemaking. This isn't the place to argue or discuss difficult topics. Get up and go to the kitchen table if any conversation begins to get heated! Otherwise, you're anchoring in negative energy in the very room which is supposed to promote love, peace, harmony, and joy. Don't let your romantic snowball spiral out of control in a bad way. Focus your attention on the loving snowball rolling in a positive direction.

Sex is the most profound form of communication!

Do's	Don'ts
1. Be Specific.	**1.Don't Discuss Negative Issues.**
How can your spouse repeat any behavior if he/she is not exactly sure what is it you like? Say, "I go crazy when you bite my buns." It's important that you communicate exactly when your partner thrills and delights you.	Never discuss downbeat matters. Never link intense angry or depressing emotions with your bed. It will only trigger harmful reactions. Nip this one in the bud, leaping out of bed if upset, mad, or anxious.
2. Be Constructive.	**2. Don't Bombard your Partner.**
Whenever you make a request for a change, use helpful and positive phrasing. Instead of saying, "Let's go slow right now." Use I-statements: "I feel a little rushed, honey." Take several seconds to think and rephrase your request for a better chance of success.	Never tell your partner he/she has to improve in a dozen areas. Because that only overwhelms or demotivates. Take one issue at a time. Resolve them. Let the new decision sink in. Wait a few days then broach other issues. It's a two-way street.
3. Be Generous.	**3. Don't be Offensive.**
Compliment your partner's good points. Make them feel like he/she is number one on the totem pole in your life. This should come naturally from love. The cliché, 'love yourself first,' is key.	Never use vulgar, distasteful, unpleasant, or degrading words. Never complain that you hate x, y, or z. Each couple must decide these boundaries for themselves.
4. Be Honest.	**4. Don't Hassle or Nag.**
Emotional dishonesty leads to feelings of anger or resentment. A sweetly-worded, sincere request will most likely be taken in the spirit in which it was given. Watch your tone of voice so it matches your body language.	Nagging doesn't work. It makes matters worse. Usually, our requests take a while to sink in, so wait a few days before bringing it up again. Either resolve, compromise or accept the situation and move on.

Create Your Rules Now:

I've listed a few to get you started. Write new rules that come to mind right away. Implement them right away and you'll notice more peaceful interactions.

Do's	Don'ts
1. _____	1. _____
_____	_____
_____	_____
2. _____	2. _____
_____	_____
_____	_____
3. _____	3. _____
_____	_____
_____	_____

For a greater understanding of what communication styles works best with your spouse or boyfriend, please check out my website: wisewords4women. com. It will announce when my next ebook, *Stoking the Coals of Communication: How NLP Fires Up your Relationship,* will be available. Unlock these secrets for better rapport with your lover.

To discover your partner's perspective, complete the following simple exercise. Once you uncover their unique communication style, you 'll get better results by using words or phrases that are in sync with them. Do what makes them feel more secure, valued, and attractive. Learn to touch your partner how he or she feels most loved.

Designate who will be A and and who will be B. Partner A begins. Cover up your answers with a sheet of paper. Write down the top three ways your partner makes you feel most loved, valued, and appreciated. Then, write down the top three actions you carry out to show affection. Don't peek.

Partner A:

Your favorite ways Person B makes you feel loved:	List what you do to make Person B feel good:
1) _____	1) _____
2) _____	2) _____
3) _____	3) _____

Before looking at the answers given above, Partner B writes down the top three ways that your mate makes you feel loved and how do you show your that he or she is loved, valued, and appreciated.

Partner B:

Your favorite ways Person A makes you feel loved:	List what you do to make Person B feel good:
1) _____	1) _____
2) _____	2) _____
3) _____	3) _____

Okay, now for the big reveal. Uncover your answers and compare. What did you learn? Great! For some couples, their answers match fairly well. Others had no clue. Sometimes we tap into our perspective without discovering what the other person prefers. It's worth the effort now to see what your partner likes.

Decide what you're going to do with this –perhaps new and revealing—information. For instance, you feed your partner chicken soup when she's sick because that's how you feel loved. Now you learn that she prefers tomato basil soup instead. Now you've learned how to offer a different way to comfort and care. That's a bonus! (The soup is just a metaphor, okay?)

How Do You Resolve Conflict?

In any live-in or long-term relationships, there are going to be tense moments and adverse situations that occasionally arise. How you decide to handle these in advance and how well you stick to the plan determines the quality of your relationship. Of course, these examples work both ways. Nobody is immune to making mistakes from time to time. Let's begin.

EXAMPLE A:

You're a married woman named Lucy, and you have worked your way up in the real estate business. As a respected developer with several commercial properties under your belt, you generate a respectable monthly cash flow. You bring your husband, Melvin, to a business conference where he has a few too many drinks.

You overhear him at the other table, laughing, as he tells a particular sexist joke that you've asked him not to tell colleagues. Several people give him dirty looks while a third verbally attacks him.

Possible Reactions:

Clearly, there is a host of options. What would you do? Do you:

1. Saunter over slowly, loop your arm through his, and walk off, claiming you want to get a drink together?
2. Apologize for his joke-telling abilities and announce he can't hold his liquor as well as you.
3. Let him struggle with the consequences on his own, which may further embarrass you if he tries to rationalize his behavior or worse, continue with additional joke-telling.
4. Grab him by his collar and yell, "We're leaving now, Mel!"

The ride back to your hotel room is a quiet one until you arrive in the parking lot, where you no longer contain your anger, "What in the hell were you thinking telling that joke when I've asked you before not to repeat it?"

"Uh, uh … I forget, honey. Come on, lots of people laughed and the men thought it was hilarious. I don't know why you get so worked up about a dirty joke," Melvin says.

You feel incensed, ready to foam at the mouth, and your hands clench into fists. "Mel, I'm never taking you to a conference again!"

Melvin extends both hands outward, flicking his fingers. "Well, good. I hate coming to these things anyway!"

Certainly, there are smoother ways to handle this sort of situation. Many people become irritated, angry, and obnoxious when they're being attacked or when they're intoxicated. It's never a good idea to discuss negative, potentially explosive issues until both parties are sober and alert.

The clear-headed person should raise the white flag. End the argument. Retreat. Go to bed. In this case, you realize he's had too much to drink. The best course of action is the most obvious. You get to your hotel room and say firmly, "We'll discuss this in the morning when you're sober."

The real test is in the morning after breakfast and a cup of coffee. How does Mel respond to your criticism and description of his unflattering behaviors from the night before? Is he more receptive to criticism now that he's sober? Is he apologetic or does he dig his heels in more firmly?

What Do You Do Next?

Hint: Use I-Statements

1. Describe his particular upsetting behavior.
2. Explain how it made you feel.
3. Make a firm request that he does not repeat the behavior.
4. Give him a reasonable consequence if it happens again.
5. Consider not bringing him to the next work event.
6. What else might get his attention?
7. Listen to his response.
8. Agree on a plan together.

It's never a good idea to use ultimatums (until the day you're willing to follow through with drastic measures.) There are ways to soften the blow and make your point stick. At least you'll have a better chance that your spouse will listen. Of course, sometimes it's the ladies who drink too much and say something obnoxious.

Bad behavior is gender-blind.

EXAMPLE B:

Mel is very disappointed because his wife isn't engaging in sex as often as she used to. "You hardly ever initiate a roll in the sack anymore, Lucy. As a matter of fact, sometimes you act like you don't even want me to touch you."

He shrugs, looks away, and shakes his head, "I'm fed up. You promise me that you'll change, but I'm tired of waiting. Will it be another three weeks before you find time to make love again?" Mel asks his wife to check with a doctor to see if there's a hormonal problem. The battle lines have been drawn.

Doesn't Mel understand how busy your schedule has been? You've been exhausted with your job, household chores, and the children. Why two weeks ago, you made love in the middle of the night even though you were stressed at work. Doesn't that count for something?

Here Are Four Mature Ways to Respond to Criticism:

TECHNIQUE:	EXPLANATION:	EXAMPLE:
1) Paraphrase it.	Put into your own words what you believe you heard your partner say.	"So, honey, you want sex more frequently?"

2) Clarify it.	Get a clearer idea by asking specific questions.	"Do you want sex more regularly or want more time in bed together when we do make love?" How often is okay?
3) Reflect it.	State what feelings you think might be the root cause of the criticism.	"Are you saying you don't feel loved lately or are you bored with our sex life in general?"
4) Express it.	Verbalize idea and thoughts in a non-judgmental way. Take ownership when it's appropriate.	"How can I make this up to you? As soon as I'm done with my project, let's spend a romantic weekend in Sedona."

Cross-Gender Communication Styles

Now that we've reviewed a few basics, I want to share the fascinating research by Georgetown University professor, Dr. Deborah Tannen. She is a world-renowned linguist, speaker, author, and business consultant. In her book, *He Said/She Said: Women, Men and Language,* Tannen explains that the way little boys and little girls interact early in life sets the stage for a style of communication for the rest of their lives. There are common observable patterns, which have been studied by linguists and sociologists over a forty-year timeline, that show distinctive gender styles.

Dr. Tannen's books on cross-gender communication grew out of her research on how people use language in everyday conversation. Once we understand these fundamental differences, the sexes can learn to get along better and communicate more effectively, thereby reducing the frustrations and arguments. The two most asked questions Professor Tannen gets when she speaks worldwide are:

1. Why don't men like to stop and ask for directions?
2. Why do women nag?

It's a complicated subject. You will have to read her book to get the complete answer to those two questions. Professor Tannen is quite specific when it comes to discovering the source of common gender patterns of speaking.

The short answer regarding cross-gender communication is that when little girls play with other little girls, they continuously use words to achieve a level of emotional connection, often repeating what the other has said. Girls use many words when they decide what game to play: "You be the mother, and I'll be the baby." "Okay, mommy, I'm hungry. Feed me." "Here's some cookies." "Yea, cookies." During playtime, girls inevitably use the same words over and over. They also tell each other private and confidential things. Sharing secrets is how girls prefer to connect, a way to become best friends. This is a predictable and prime way that young females, ages three-six, learn to negotiate and socialize.

Equality and connection are prized attributes. If a newcomer joins the group, the others wait to see how well she fits in by listening to her. Does she use similar words? Is she willing to negotiate? Does she play fair? If so, she's accepted as an equal member of the group. If not, she's almost immediately ostracized.

When girls become women, they primarily use words to establish new friendships. Equality plays a larger role in their lives, and many become greeters and connectors in the circles they run in. How do adult women ostracize another female? A female boss in the process of hiring says, "You might find that company X is a better fit for you because of your high level of skills in area Y." Women are more likely to be indirect in their actions and words while men tend to be more direct. An adult male in a similar position might say, "This is not the right company for you to work for, but I want to thank you for coming in," shaking hands as he escorts the interviewee out the door.

Little boys playing with other boys grow up doing physical activities together, using fewer words, to establish a bond. Typically, there is a clear hierarchy based on physical prowess or one's ability to lead, commanding the others to build a fort. One strong boy may announce, "I wanna play king of the hill." This leader may bully a newcomer until the other subjugates and follows the group rules. If someone suggests tag football and the group agrees, the first leader now subjugates his original role because he lost that particular battle. When a bully emerges, then there is an inevitable fight and a temporary winner.

Bonding happens during the act of competition. Activities such as wrestling or gaming establish friendships, which takes precedence over talking to each other. Status is more important than equality. When they do talk to each other, they seldom look directly at their friends because they are usually involved in an action. It's the competitive activity that bonds them, not the words.

When boys become men, they follow similar hierarchical patterns. There are leaders and followers. Of course, men learn how to give eye contact and talk respectfully for the most part; however, they never want to be put in a one-down position like when they were pushed around as a boy. Men will do almost anything, even stop talking altogether, if it means saving face.

Consequently, adult males evaluate and talk to women in a way that makes sense to them. If they perceive a put-down, they attack. Men maintain a sense of hierarchy by competing verbally or comparing their financial status.

Where connection, equality, and negotiation are important for women, it's hierarchy, competition, and status that are essential for men.

Because of this worldview, men have a distinct, perhaps a skewed, vision of communication. For instance, the administrative head of a hospital responsible for evaluating a group of new doctors gave the only female intern a low score. When she asked why, he said, "You don't know as much as your counterparts."

"My test scores show that I outshine 94% of my colleagues. So, what makes you say that?"

"Because you ask so many questions," he responds. Apparently, the male interns never put themselves in a one-down position, especially in front of others. They wouldn't typically ask a question for fear of appearing less informed, thereby losing status. Females come from a background of valued equality and negotiation; therefore, they have no problem admitting they don't know everything. By the way, which doctor would you prefer having in the long run?

Similarly, women miss the point of cross-gender communication. While driving, a wife asks her husband, "Would you like to stop for something to eat? Mel says, "No," and keeps on driving. Twenty minutes later, Lucy lashes out and says how mad she is because he is not considerate of her needs. "Why didn't you tell me that you wanted to grab a bite?" Mel asks. "If I knew you wanted to, I would've stopped. Why do you play this game with me?"

Lucy thinks they should negotiate and discuss the options because that's how she connects and feels close, like when she was a little girl. "You should have at least talked to me about it," she insists. "Instead, you give me a one-word answer." "Now hold on, honey, I answered your question honestly. I wasn't hungry." Mel finally snaps, "Don't expect me to read your mind. You're being ridiculous. End of story." He gives her the silent treatment the next two hours. Well, you see how this dynamic plays out over and over again in personal relationships. It's a vicious cycle. There is less frustration once we step into the other person's shoes.

The point of this discussion is to show that men and women, in general, have different communication styles, which affect how they perceive their partner. Men can learn to understand why women enjoy sharing details about their day, revealing gossip along the way. When a woman mentions a problem at work, she is frustrated when her husband only responds by offering a solution.

She'll figure out how to solve a problem later. She wants to know he's listening to her because that's how she feels intimate and connected. Sharing secrets also make her feel close.

Women, too, can learn to appreciate a man's position. Your boyfriend feels close when you're watching a football game together. Once you understand that your husband doesn't have to look directly at you to listen, you may be less frustrated when he lays on the couch with his arms over his eyes. Some men listen better without the distraction of looking at a woman, especially if the subject is deeply emotional or important. Once a woman is aware of this, she can be more forgiving of his unconventional style. On the flip side, a woman can learn to ask direct questions or simply make a request.

Be sensitive to different styles of communication. Men can be more direct, depending on the context, but that doesn't mean he doesn't love you. Women can be more indirect, but that can be a form of caring. By the way, men are typically less direct when it comes to making an apology because he thinks that puts him in a one-down position. A man would rather send flowers than say the actual words, "I'm sorry," because that implies guilt and he doesn't want to appear weak or feel like he owes the other person something. Remember, competition is essential to him. He hates to be in a one-down position. So accept his apology and move on.

Enough about words and communication. Go out. Have fun. Get a drink and listen to some music to celebrate. Sometimes being together without any words is an ideal connection. Hold hands. Sit. Listen. Be content.

Good job! You finished
Week Six Challenge:
Strengthening Cross-Gender Communication

CHAPTER 7

WEEK SEVEN CHALLENGE: DISCOVERING COMPATIBLE CHEMISTRY

This week you will find ways to integrate mental, physical, emotional (and perhaps spiritual) dimensions to achieve heightened sexual pleasure. Today's exercises are designed to help you look at your sensuality and discover your capacity for love, intimacy, orgasm, romance, and more.

Take the Week Seven Quiz:

1. What do you want from your relationship?
2. What do you want in bed? How important is a physical release?
3. Is real passion more important than frequency?
4. Does your sexual appetite usually match your lover's?
5. Is your spouse or mate domineering in the bedroom?
6. On a scale from one to ten, do you feel comfortable getting your partner to meet your needs? Why or why not?

Use this as a catalyst for a serious conversation. Jot down your answers, thoughts, feelings, and ideas:

His: _____

_____

_____

_____

_____

_____

Hers: _____

_____

_____

_____

_____

How Big a Role Does Self-Confidence Play?

Bigger than we think. A great relationship boils down to self-esteem and communication and perhaps our willingness to compromise. What works for one couple does not fit for another. Do what feels right and discard the rest.

Anne of Tulsa, Oklahoma sent me a letter after reading my first book. She writes:

> "I have never felt as though I know enough to perform masterfully in bed. So I am ready to learn... I want to be more relaxed and self-confident. To be very blunt, I don't masturbate. Personally, I find the thought obscene. Is masturbation absolutely necessary for self-discovery?
>
> I know that I would love to explore every inch of my boyfriend's body...Can you recommend how to really drive a man crazy? I want to know what I am doing, and

I want to know that what I am doing will satisfy him... I know that half of my problem is that I don't 'feel' sexy at all. It's not that I don't 'feel' sexy upon occasion, just that I don't think I look sexy.

I admit, I am timid. Not afraid of sex, but afraid of experimenting. I am afraid that he will think I am psycho or weird. He seems hesitant to talk about sex, or anything really intimate for that matter...yeah, the obvious answer is to tell him what I am thinking, but again, he seems too uncomfortable when we discuss anything like that. I don't quite know what that signifies."

Frankly, Anne asks many of the same questions that I hear from other women. Her comments show that both genders have doubts and insecurities about their ability to perform. Perhaps it's a matter of maturity. Many people are shy about discussing sex and that's why couples benefit from a book they complete together.

The good way to gain self-confidence is to proceed with all the interactive exercises in this manual, even if the material pushes couples beyond their comfort zone.

Remember, there's no substitute for love, respect, and basic kindness. In our chemical-oriented quick-fix society, we expect instant gratification. If used sparingly, the sex-enhancing drugs available today are helpful if needed. However, when a little blue pill is being targeted for young men in their twenties and thirties, I think the pharmaceutical companies have gone overboard. Clearly, a small percentage of people in different stages of their lives need extra help now and then.

For most young males, a warm breeze is all it takes to get them aroused. For the mature crowd, be cautious about using any prescription medication and do so under a doctor's orders. Long-term studies of the side effects have not yet been done with the newer drugs out in today's market. Even then, do your research. Go to any multi-drug interaction checker online. Enough said.

Is Your Chemistry Compatible?

If you're like most people, you've selected a spouse or partner based on a physical attraction in the beginning. Did you know that there are chemicals in your body called pheromones (pronounced fair-moans) that cause the opposite sex to be attracted to you? All animals have them. Presumably, they were created for all species to survive. Nature takes over.

The average person, it has been reported, feels a chemical attraction well before the third date. Once released by your body, this chemical substance influences the physiology and behavior of your mate. There are even perfumes with the intention of attracting a mate! In my opinion, it's always best to go with your own natural, clean scent! Your chemically-compatible partner will love it!

What physical characteristics were you most attracted to when you first met each other?

His: _____

_____

_____

_____

_____

_____

Hers: _____

_____

_____

_____

_____

_____

Compare the two lists. Men typically go for breasts, legs, or butt while women usually say, the eyes, face, or overall body type.

There are many scientific studies about the chemical changes in the human body throughout the duration of a romantic relationship. Being in love results in chemical changes in your body. Admittedly, some heavy duty chemical reactions are firing off in our bodies when we first fall in love— it's magical and the best feeling in the world.

Once that spark is there, we start to sense the emotional bond. When love fades, for whatever reason, it's difficult to create good chemistry again. What characteristics were added to your list as you got to know each other better?

His: _____

_____

_____

_____

_____

_____

Hers: _____

_____

_____

_____

_____

_____

Your sex life might have started out with a bang and then leveled out to a passionate steadiness that is wonderful. Or it could've started out slow and built up over time, with trial and error, to a similar level of heightened sexual pleasure. Great no matter how you got there.

Discover Your Psychological Comfort Level

You must be comfortable with your body and the pleasure it can give you. Whether you do this through masturbation or with a partner is your choice. What counts is that you're emotionally complete, relaxed, and whole as a sexual individual. If this remains a stumbling block, then try the various suggestions and exercises in this workbook until you are comfortable with your sexuality.

Reading and talking to others about human sexuality also helps. Be careful what you choose to put into your mind. Like the saying goes, "Garbage in, garbage out." Why put trash or degrading images into your head? Sex can directly serve lust, or it can transcend desire and merge two souls. Remember, what you think about most often manifests. Express your romantic love and watch the magic expand.

Write down your answers separately and add up your points. Understand where your partner is coming from when he/she rates you. Realize no human is meant to score perfectly. Be honest. What you figure out now can make a huge difference in the future. Discuss. Be open with each other.

Take the Psychological Profile Quiz:

Consider one is Totally Unlike You or Your Situation while ten is Most Like You. On a scale from one to ten points, rate the following statements:

_____1. I talk to my partner easily about a variety of subjects.

_____2. When we talk about a sensitive subject or argue, we come to a resolution in a reasonable manner in a fair amount of time.

_____3. I consider my partner one of my best friends.

_____4. If I am feeling low or blue, my partner knows what to do or say.

_____5. I have fun with my spouse or mate when we're not in bed.

_____6. We enjoy at least two to three mutual interests and have similar tastes in entertainment, e.g., hiking, movies, reading, sports, travel, cooking, music, dancing.

_____7. My partner makes me feel special on a regular basis.

_____8. I can act silly around my partner, and I feel totally at ease. My partner provides a safe space and lets me be real, accepting and loving me for who I am.

_____9. Generally speaking, we have similar ideas about money and agree on how to handle finances as a couple.

_____10. My partner listens to me when I ask for his/her undivided attention. I believe my viewpoint is being heard, even if we don't always agree on everything.

Add Up Total Points:

10-40 points indicate LOW COMPATIBILITY. A gloomy relationship at best, this person might be on your 'Nix List.' I suspect you're involved in an arranged and emotionally distant relationship. Even if the sex is good, you don't experience close ties at other times. You might ask yourself these questions: Am I afraid of intimacy? Why am I spending my time with this person? Do yourself (and your partner) a favor. Say, goodbye. Read my ebook, Love Him or Leave Him, found on my website called wisewords4women.com so you can be prepared for this transition. Then move forward. It's easier than you think.

41-75 points indicate MEDIUM COMPATIBILITY. Does the word ambiguous ring a bell? How about noncommittal? This couple is on the "Fix List." Probably your relationship works alright most of the time. Still, you feel the struggle to connect on a deeper level than, "What's for dinner, honey?" Perhaps you're bored. You need to recharge your batteries and see if the relationship improves. You only have control over your behavior. You can start by being more loving and less critical and see what happens. This works both ways. Do you want to work this much or not?

76-99 points indicate HIGH COMPATIBILITY. Wow! Your mate belongs on the Keeper List. You two have more going for you than most couples. You have made it through many years already, or you have the potential to last through thick and thin. I bet your partner makes you feel happy, alive, valued, and appreciated. This is as good as it gets. (100 points indicate there's a good probability you're delusional!) And you're likely to be disappointed for the rest of your life. Nobody's perfect.

Do you feel a little more romantic now? Be adventurous. Try something new!

An Erotic-Discovery Exercise:

Today, I recommend a fun study of textures and sensations created by a series of touches on various places on your partner's body. Let the fun and games begin!

Gather a variety of textural items around the house:

Wet washrag	(wrapped with ice cubes)
Piece of fur	(perhaps on a coat)
Baby powder	(baby oil at least)
Beanbag	(or coffee beans)
Sandpaper	(fine and coarse)
Marbles	(smooth round objects)
Neck Warmer	(microwavable item)
Rose pedals	(select any flower)
Feather	(peacock or bird feather)

Follow These Simple Steps:

1. Lay out all of your objects (six to ten items) in front of both people.
2. Ask your spouse to turn his or her arm over, palm faced upward.
3. Now have your partner close his or her eyes.
4. Select an object.

5. Rub it, using medium pressure at first, on your partner's forearm.

6. Ask your partner to guess which object you selected.

7. Continue until you've selected most or all of the objects.

Now switch places. The giver becomes the receiver. Simple game. Some couples choose to play this game as a part of their foreplay routine. Select these objects or more over various regions of the body with your partner's permission. I recommend letting the receiver decide if he or she wants to keep eyes open or closed. Be creative. Use a feather and rose pedals together to stroke your lover all over.

K-I-S-S-I-N-G

Do you remember the song, "Jack & Jill, sitting in a tree, k-i-s-s-i-n-g. First came love, then came marriage, then came Johnny in a baby carriage?"

This week would not be complete if we didn't talk about kissing. Kissing is a particular mode of connecting with your partner. A definite turn-on. You haven't been kissed adequately if your spouse hasn't kissed your neck, forehead, breasts, butt, toes, back, earlobe, or behind the knees.

Go on an all-over-the-body kissing spree!

While there are exceptions to every rule, a good kisser makes a good lover. We all have personal quirks. Most females enjoy slow, soft, kisses, lingering long enough for satisfaction yet leaving them wanting more.

If your man needs a little improvement in this area, start by telling him to follow your lead. Of course, it's great when a guy gets training from an experienced woman who knows her stuff, preferably as a teenager. Teenagers are usually more willing to experiment.

Kissing is an essential part of foreplay. Kissing shows that your partner cares. It also helps rev up your partner's sexual motor. In your opinion, is there a relation between kissing styles and how someone makes love? Or do kisses directly reveal your partner's mood at the time? This list contains six basic kissing types:

- Short, closed-mouth pecks
- Soft, open-mouthed without tongue
- Sweet, open-mouthed French kisses
- Hard, open-mouthed without tongue
- Hard, open-mouthed French kisses
- Playful tongue flicking

Unless you're a very young teenager, nobody likes too wet, too hard, or too sloppy types. A few pecks before a sexual encounter may signal that your partner is interested. It's also a nice gesture as part of the after-glow.

An open-mouthed kiss packs more of an emotional punch than a briefer peck, sweetening up the situation. A warm, moist mouth just feels right during any part of a love-making session.

French kisses seem to be the meat-and-potatoes of foreplay and help stir loving sensations. They're a terrific lead-up to sex and also a way to show you care about your partner during intercourse as well.

A hard kiss indicates the sex-play has reached a level of intensity. When mixed with other styles, these can be received well. Some kisses become symbolic of what is happening in the vagina. A deep tongue is like a second penetration, imitating what goes on below. Typically, one party is the recipient of their lover's tongue, enveloping it entirely. Switching up who gives more tongue is a matter of personal preference like so many other things in life.

Playful tongue-flicks seem to be the sweetest. When playfulness becomes a part of the norm, a couple is more likely to try new things. By doing so, you keep sex from becoming stale and repetitive.

All in all, there are infinite ways to kiss someone you love. It's different every time. Lumping styles into six categories provide a springboard for discussion in case you want to broach the subject with someone you love. Mixing and matching your kisses to your love-making impacts the sensations so you can enjoy sex to its fullest.

CONGRATULATIONS!
You've completed the
Week Seven Challenge:
Discovering Compatible Chemistry

CHAPTER 8

FINDING YOUR ORAL
INTIMACY QUOTIENT

What do men and women really want?

To be clear, this isn't the stuff of X-rated movies. This chapter explores a sensitive topic in a no-nonsense way. It helps you overcome shyness, and provides inspiration for using oral sex to reach a new degree of sexual intimacy that many couples rarely achieve. If you feel too self-conscious to discuss oral sexuality with your partner, read on.

This chapter will help you communicate clearly about your needs and embrace your partner's sexual desires. Men are also encouraged to learn what pleases women by asking for feedback or asking questions in a non-intimidating manner.

Straight Talk About The Gift of Tongues

What are we talking about here? Oral sex is a sexual activity in which the genitals of one partner are stimulated by the mouth of the other. Fellatio is what is performed on a penis and cunnilingus is conducted on a woman's vagina. This section will primarily cover fellatio and cunnilingus, while also pointing to a range of techniques covered in oral eroticism.

Ask a happily married man, "Do you enjoy oral sex with your wife?" Many will respond, "Oh, that stopped the minute she walked down the aisle." Sadly, there is some truth in humor. In a ladies locker room, I once overheard a woman say, "To tell the truth, I don't give my husband blow jobs anymore. I just did that to get him to marry me." To me, she's a fraud! And that's no joke.

Men and women need information in advance to dodge embarrassing situations in the bedroom. With simple guidance, these potentially difficult predicaments can be avoided. Women can understand men's unique gift of expressing passion and strength. As a woman releases vital nerve force, her partner opens up to deeper feelings. Every nerve impulse and muscle movement stems from energy channels—chakras that correlate to meridian points flowing along the spine—and help heighten sexual sensations when they are unblocked and transmitted to another person. Men also express love through their physical energy. Reaching states of passion can be enhanced with oral stimulation, which can become an exceptionally gratifying act between loving partners.

Do you or a loved one have a major block against oral sex? What if you're in love with someone who requires oral stimulation to be satisfied? This manual not only provides a clear guide to those who would like to achieve heightened pleasure and increase their Oral IQ (Intimacy Quotient), it also offers a variety of practical solutions to overcome obstacles as well as a few tried-and-true techniques.

Many couples have lost interest in oral sex or simply don't know how to rekindle the romantic spark. Over and over again, I hear both men and women complain that sex is too often meaningless, mechanical, or not worth the effort. Working couples never seem to have time for each other. Often those who live together admit they aren't as satisfied as they would like to be.

Breaking Down The Barriers

For a man to admit he's never tried oral sex is not macho; a woman who admits it is considered unsophisticated. Mild qualms can be overcome, of course, but what if you have a major block against it? The object of oral sex is to achieve greater sexual satisfaction and a feeling of closeness with a partner. To accomplish this, both partners must feel comfortable.

First of all, nothing is wrong with you just because you find certain sex practices unpalatable. You're entitled to preferences. It's only a dilemma if your aversion bothers your partner. If your mate is fine with it, then no worries. Certainly, couples can have a satisfying sex life without oral gratification. However, you can teach an old dog new tricks. After a dozen years together, many couples try new activities.

There's a deep-seated primal connection when two lovers engage in oral sex. If you're reading this now, you must be curious or have a desire to learn more about it. The benefits are overwhelming. Sex is the glue that keeps relationships together. It can't be the only ingredient, but for many, it's an important one.

Unfortunately, when someone is unaware of their sexual preference or uneducated about the techniques of oral sex, they can easily find themselves in uncomfortable situations. Laura, an eighteen-year-old virgin, threw up on her wedding night when her husband forced her to give him a blow job. He didn't offer any instruction or compassion. In fact, she had no clue what was about to happen. He pushed his penis into her mouth and demanded that she suck hard.

She was scared and intimidated by a much older man, who obviously wasn't sensitive to his new wife's situation. Years later, Laura was able to overcome this obstacle. Men too can have embarrassing moments. Many know very little about a woman's oral sexual desires.

How comfortable each partner feels depends on their upbringing, their religious background, their gender, and their personal experiences with oral sex. Discover your attitude toward oral sex. A learned restrictive belief system, emotional injuries that haven't been forgiven, or a lack of healthy practices can cause a sexual shut-down. Take extra care if tensions have built up from repeated guilt, denial, abuse, or repression of emotions. Seek counseling as needed.

Let's focus on useful suggestions for better sex and practical insights. The advantages outweigh the disadvantages. Stop and think about it. Oral sex can be:

- ☐ erotic
- ☐ easily accessible
- ☐ pregnancy proof
- ☐ fun and exciting
- ☐ effective
- ☐ a learn-able skill
- ☐ gratifying
- ☐ intimate

Oral Sex Carries More Gratifying Features:

1. Adds variety to your sex life
2. Prolongs lovemaking sessions
3. Enriches private moments
4. Stimulates erogenous zones
5. Helps relax body tension
6. Excites the senses
7. Releases stress
8. Fulfills innate primitive needs
9. Helps foster a close connection
10. Requires less physical energy than intercourse

Three decades ago, Ronna Rommey, in her book *Giving Time a Chance*, explains, "We are currently in the age of intimacy." How would you describe the age we live in today? Some say it's a marriage of the digital age and the age of spirituality. Here's hoping we can blend these generations together for heightened pleasure and peaceful interactions with our loved ones.

Everyone longs for contentment, a sense of being special, and sexual satisfaction; yet for many, this has proved to be an elusive goal. That's what this chapter is all about. It goes beyond the physical dimension—including mental, emotional, and ethereal aspects of oral lovemaking—to secrets of lovers who know how to make the most of their private moments.

After getting feedback from people who read my first book, *How to Have Multiple Orgasms*, it was clear that readers found a level of heightened emotional intimacy could often be achieved by combining oral sex with intercourse. This creates one of the most profound and intimate feelings that can occur between two people.

A person's connection with their partner may be impacted by the individual's self-esteem, personal beliefs, knowledge of their body, and a willingness to learn. Oral sex is a delightful technique to achieve physical, emotional, psychological and metaphysical bliss.

For some, oral lovemaking can be scary. Unfortunately, many women and some men believe oral sex is vulgar. This belief causes women to be sexually inhibited and men to be frustrated. Fortunately, both genders can reinvent themselves.

Passion is complicated. It takes chemistry, confidence and charisma and the right information. Sex educators agree that couples who practice oral sex on a regular basis enjoy lovemaking the most. Remember, roughly 90% of sexually-active men and women have engaged in some degree of oral gratification.

Without extra encouragement, however, some lovers never learn to enjoy oral lovemaking. For those who want to make the most of their intimate moments, this chapter helps readers achieve sexual satisfaction and greater closeness. Obtain a clear picture of your sexual needs. Because of cultural and societal influences, few men and women understand what they need to be sexually and emotionally satisfied.

This section helps readers to take an in-depth look at a sensitive subject. Look within. Complete a sexual-emotional inventory. Try a few new activities.

What Are the Six Steps to Oral Pleasure?

1. <u>Obtain a clear picture of your own sexual needs.</u> Because of cultural and societal influences, few men and women understand what they really need to be sexually and emotionally satisfied. This section helps readers to look within themselves and do a sexual-emotional inventory.

2. <u>Create a R-I-P-E relationship.</u> Real sexual companionship occurs only after a couple develops a solid foundation. A good relationship is a mature and healthy one developed over time. Remember R-I-P-E stands for respect, intimacy, passion, and emotional support. It requires a mature give-and-take mindset. Extraordinary passion stems from deep-seated love.

3. <u>Discover your sexual passions.</u> Find your true sexual self without depending on anyone else for an answer. Discover through trial and error what pleases you and what pleases your partner. This introspection helps with the decision-making process. Next, readers develop an action mindset.

4. <u>Talk, Talk, Talk.</u> Design a communication strategy and share it with your partner. Once you get in the habit of talking openly to your partner about your sexual needs, the more comfortable you will become. Consequently, there's enhanced enjoyment. This section also includes a helpful list of Do's and Don'ts.

5. <u>Practice, Practice, Practice.</u> The section below will provide you with approaches to giving and receiving. It describes seventeen oral activities—ten for men and seven for women—to increase sexual pleasure.

6. <u>Get feedback from your partner.</u> Respect the learning process. Discover your partner's needs and desires through actual experimentation. Positive reinforcement between lovers is especially important to safely determine your own comfort zone.

These six steps comprise a supportive model to achieve a life-affirming and effective Oral IQ (Intimacy Quotient). Both men and women can become more competent in fulfilling their partner's needs. Open communication helps any couple develop mutual understanding, respect, and acceptance.

What Do Women Really Want?

Why do some women crave oral sex and other women shrink from it? I believe this goes back to their upbringing as well as their first encounter with oral sex. What was your first-time experience with oral pleasuring like? Do you see a connection between that early experience and how you behave now? Many think oral sex is crude; some women don't know what they want. Unless women feel secure and loved by their mate, some lovers simply don't enjoy giving or receiving orally.

Sometimes women share their most intimate secrets and their need for oral sex with a best friend instead of their lover. I overheard these comments at a beauty salon: "I love to get and give pleasure at the same time. I like giving my partner enjoyment when he's just stepped out of the shower. I enjoy having my man lick and kiss the insides of my legs until I can't stand it and I beg him to get inside me." If you're sensitive about this issue, then keep reading. If you're a man, learn why women seem hesitant about giving or receiving oral sex. Taking the taboos out of oral sex is possible if you take it one step at a time. The book, *Oragenitalism*, is probably one of the first books published about the subject back in 1969.

Yes, the year seems more than coincidental.

The following two lists were created from actual quotes and paraphrases from an anonymous survey. These are the responses I got from both genders:

<u>WOMEN'S LIST</u>

Reasons Women Don't Like Giving Fellatio:

1. I don't like to be forced to give head.
2. I'm afraid he'll come in my mouth.

3. He stinks. I mean, literally, he has bad body odor.
4. I feel like he's controlling my behavior.
5. It's exhausting and hurts my mouth. It feels unnatural like I'm going against nature.
6. It's against my religion and I feel guilty.
7. It's messy and disgusting.
8. Men act like my throat is made of leather. I can't last an hour.
9. My guy takes forever to reach orgasm. Frankly, I get bored.
10. He's not happy with my performance unless I fake eagerness.
11. Why isn't doing it enough for him?
12. It makes me feel whorish. (Don't gag me!)

MEN'S LIST

Reasons Men Don't Want Giving Cunnilingus

1. It's messy.
2. She smells bad.
3. She tastes awful.
4. My tongue gets tired.
5. How long am I expected to do this?
6. I don't think it's natural. Is my tongue a pleasuring device?
7. She'd rather me go down on her than intercourse.
8. It makes me feel inadequate like I'm not good enough.
9. It's too slow. She takes forever to reach orgasm.
10. It's too fast. She comes too quickly and then she's tired.
11. She treats me like I'm some sort of a machine.
12. It's disgusting to me. Don't ask me to explain it.
13. She expects me to be gung-ho about it.

What are the common reasons that both men and women gave for not enjoying oral sex? Both lists include the mess, taste, and smell.

Sink or Swim?

For many people, cleanliness is a big issue. Where do people feel the most sanitary? In water. Viola! Putting two and two together, I realized some folks could break the barrier by combining oral sex with a bathtub, a swimming pool, or a warm hot tub. The result is worth the effort. Most couples love to hug and kiss in a pool, where they feel more relaxed, especially when the relationship is new.

Even if you don't live in a sunny environment, surely you can find a remote motel with a moderately dark area. Adventurous souls make love al fresco (outdoors) now and then. Most couples prefer the dark for this activity, but brave lovers engage anytime in the privacy of their backyard.

After some frivolous foreplay in the pool, have the male sit on the top step with his butt in the water. The female kneels in front of him, where she can easily reach his penis with her mouth. Her mate has to be clean by now, even if he tastes a little like chlorine. In this playful arena, most people relax a little and are more open to experimentation.

If your lover is inexperienced in giving head (or this is her first time), be patient. Don't force it. Let the woman try a few things and tell her what feels good. Be definite and concrete. Tell her, "Put your fingers around the base while you suck my tip." Don't ask for too much in the early learning stages.

One of the biggest mistakes a man can make is to demand more when his partner says she's had enough. This anchors in negative feelings and makes your partner less likely to participate later.

Even if it's only been a few minutes, tell her how much you enjoyed it. The next time will more likely be longer. You can shape her behavior by being positive and supportive during the learning process. Let her try different things and simply tell her what feels good and what doesn't. Use I-statements. "I like it when you hold me firmly."

Some couples use a scale from one to ten to give feedback. It's fast, easy, and better than saying "Yuck!" If she loves you, she will learn to treasure giving you delight in this way. One good turn deserves another. Now let the female take the top step (or sit on the deck of the pool) while the male remains in the water.

Again, the woman feels and smells clean, so she doesn't have as many worries. The guy usually has less anxiety because of the flexible nature of water. Allow the man to try a few different techniques; and, of course, the woman can offer valuable feedback.

Trust me; the water has a funny habit of arousing people in fresh and stimulating ways. With this technique, you can take the taboos out of oral sex.

What Do Men Really Want?

This information is derived from my Exploring the Sexual Dimensions of Your Relationship seminars and an anonymous survey. Men say the ideal oral sex partner would be:

- Enthusiastic
- Willing to learn what I like
- Willing to tell me what she likes
- Is firm, yet gentle enough not to hurt me
- Confident in how to please me
- Rarely refuses when I ask for a blow job

Many women do match what men desire and are willing to learn how to please their partner. Here are some examples what their partners like:

"My husband likes me to start at the base of his penis and kiss his manhood while he is still soft. As he stiffens, I ratchet up the speed and the firmness of my movements." Another explains, "My husband goes wild when I rub my teeth up and down his shaft." Other men hate it when they feel teeth. "Ouch! What the heck are you doing down there?" So how is a woman suppose to know what her partner likes if he never tells her? Trial and error? It's called communication folks. (Refer to chapter six.)

Obtain a Clear Picture of Your Needs

Oral lovemaking can be the most profound and intimate act between two loving individuals. In response to my questionnaire, men and women said the following: "I want my wife to lick my ears and neck during sex. A woman says, I want my lover to kiss me all over during foreplay, and I want my mate to spend more time licking and kissing my back and be a little rough. I also like it when he bites my butt gently and then massages it firmly."

In general, anxiety over sexual issues isn't as prevalent today compared to previous generations. However, both men and women have their stresses and emotions about particulars in the bedroom.

How we view sexuality is influenced by many factors: age, social media, family history, gender, sexual identity, race, ethnicity, economic status, mainstream media, entertainment venues, and sexual orientation.

It's critical to be sensitive to these differences as we think about sexuality when we're in a romantic relationship. Be gentle at first. Explain your position. Teach your partner what you like. Be patient.

I Never Met a Man ...

I never met a man who didn't enjoy a blow job. However, the women interviewed stressed the same theme over and over again. Unless they felt secure and loved by their mate, they didn't enjoy receiving or giving oral sex. Men, on the other hand, seemed somewhat frustrated by the lack of enthusiasm from their partner, unable to encourage their mate to give them more of what they needed without being perceived as overbearing. Females found controlling and domineering partners very unattractive.

Couples, please. You need to talk, talk, talk. How do you tell your partner that you want something different? Or that you want less oral sex? Verbally, a lover can direct and reinforce their mate with such things as:

> "Oh, yes, keep doing what you're doing."
> "You found the spot, again."
> "That's nice. It's different, but I like it for a change of pace."
> "Love your finger circling inside me while you suck."
> "You've got my number, babe."
> "Can we try that again?"

Unfortunately, a negative word or phrase often puts both the man and the woman on the defensive. Feelings are so fragile when it comes to sex that I recommend that if you have something significant to tell a partner, say it as honestly and as tactfully as possible. Use positive phrasing when you can.

If your partner is doing something you don't like, you could say,

> "Hold up a minute."
> "Can we move on to something else?"
> "Let's trade places."
> "I want to please you in another way now."
> "Could we go slower?"

For a longer feedback session, hold this conversation away from the bedroom. If you feel it's too difficult to say in person, write out what you want to say and hand your partner a note. Discuss its content after you both feel refreshed and content. Practice makes perfect, so be willing to experiment for a happy partnership!

This section describes seventeen oral exercises that encourage you to try new things, including the following ten fellatio and seven cunnilingus techniques both men and women can use to heighten their partner's pleasure. Oral sex is an art that can drive your lover wild! It's an art that can be improved.

Experiment with these Techniques:

- The Round Trip
- The French Kiss
- Breeze & Tease
- Lickin' & Flickin'
- The Happy Hummer
- Trumpet Lips
- The Barber Pole
- The Thumbelina Trick
- Salami Tsunami
- The Tooth Tantalizer

Get feedback from your partner early on, so you can be confident that you please him. Of course, it's obvious when a man is aroused. As discussed in chapter four, feedback is the key to successful sex! Simply ask, "On a scale from one to ten, how does this feel?" Even people who communicate well in other areas of their lives often are hesitant to talk about this sensitive issue.

Ten Fellatio Techniques:

Try these techniques. Add your favorites. Then, mix and match:

1) The Round Trip—You'll need to warm up the man before going to the sucking motion. Don't you want a warm up before he licks your clitoris? Same idea. Start at the base of the penis with a firm hand, licking from the base up in long tongue strokes until you hit about an inch from the tip.

Grasp firmly enough to control your movements, but not too much to cut off the blood flow. Do this from a different angle by turning your head to the left and right periodically. Eventually, you will suck from the base to the tip using the roof of your mouth or the back of your throat as end points. Move your hand up and down about half way up his shaft while doing this.

Your hands will meet your lips when you move in an upward direction. Then your hands will move in a downward direction while your lips meet the tip of the penis at the same time. Use whatever speed and grip intensity he prefers. Each male is a little different. You'll learn what he likes. Keep a steady rhythm in the beginning until you feel his penis getting engorged with blood. Then quicken the pace and intensity of sucking until he climaxes. He can let you know by placing his hand gently on your head to indicate what tempo he needs at any moment. Follow his lead.

2) The French Kiss—Using a similar technique as a French kiss, use your tongue and lips to caress and love him. If you look directly at him while doing this, it's a big turn-on for men. Kiss his penis like you would touch his lips. Do this in a caring manner, and he will feel the love. It's not always about the swift suck off.

3) Breeze & Tease—After you've licked your man, blow cool air on him. This works great in between long, slow sucking motions. Besides, your mouth may need some rest in between sucking. Give yourself a break! Also, men want to be teased at first just like you do. So bring him closer to climax and then slow it back down. It gives him more pleasure in the long run if he has to wait once or twice. If he says he can't hold on, then go for the gold! Trial and error is the best way for a couple to learn what satisfies each other.

4) Lickin' & Flickin'—Feel free to lick his scrotum and testicles as part of an oral sex treat. You will blow his mind. Try licking his manhood from the bottom upwards and give his penis tip a gentle, flick of the tongue. Lick some more and do more flicks on the tip like he would your clitoris. Some men love this. Others are too sensitive. Tread carefully.

5) The Happy Hummer—A unique man may enjoy you engulfing his penis and after a few head-moving strokes add some actual humming. Hum your favorite song. Get feedback later. It's just a change of pace.

6) Trumpet Lips: Have you ever played a brass or wind musical instrument?

If so, you know instinctively what to do. Otherwise, pretend to make trumpet sounds. Otherwise, try tooting with your lips put together on the top two inches of his penis, moving with small strokes just on his tip.

7) The Barber Pole—Lick and suck, swirling your tongue and lips around his penis like the stripes on a barber's pole while sucking. You might have to be in a different position than usual for this one. Put his penis in your mouth as far as it can go and on your way up, feel free to turn your head around in both directions, sucking as you go.

Stimulate the head because that's where most of his nerve endings are present. But back off if he gets too sensitive. Ask him to tell you when if he wants you to slow down or speed up. Does he want you to suck harder or less intense? While we usually can read his body reactions, we can't read his mind.

8) The Thumbelina Trick—This technique just combines giving a blow job at the same time you stick a thumb (or finger) in his anus. Move gently at first, using a circling motion. Notice if he likes it, then go deeper. Pull your finger or thumb out the moment he starts to come.

9) Salami Tsunami—This is simply a full out sucking off a man hard from start to finish. Holding your hand at the base, move your wet lips and closed mouth around his penis and suck as if you're sucking on your favorite ice cream cone. Suck at a quicker or slower pace, harder or less intense, depending on the preferences of your partner. A majority of men prefer you absorb his entire shaft rather than just the tip. Your partner will be physically spent quickly.

You might want to lead up to this one since this is his most sensitive area. Warm him up first. Our mouths have a unique ability to be wet, warm, and succulent. A vagina can't suck like a vacuum. An oral sex orgasm is mind-blowing for both men and women alike.

10) The Tooth Tantalizer—Only for the brave at heart, this technique involves you gently, very gently, running your teeth up and down the shaft of his already wet penis. Don't go near the tip of his penis until you're ready for the real long, hard, swift strokes while sucking. Hold his testicles firmly while you do this. Mix and match any two techniques listed here.

Typically, you'll want to start at the base of a man's penis and work your way upwards. Let your partner determine the pace and the intensity of the sucking motion. Most men like it hard and relatively fast as they get closer to climax.

Seven Cunnilingus Techniques:

I hear it from both sexes: I want more oral gratification. One seminar participant exclaimed, "I require lots of tongue from a man, but how do I ask for more?" A woman can use the direct approach: "I usually like at least ten minutes of oral sex before penetration." Here are a few techniques for your partner to try:

1. Smooth Sailing—Warm up your lover with slow wet kisses. It's best to kiss other parts of her body first to allow her to picture what you're going to do later. Perhaps kiss and tongue near her belly button or inner thighs. Once you reach her vagina, she should be wet already. If not, no worries. You can kiss and tongue her, using circular motions to start. Use steady, rhythmic movements with your mouth and tongue.

Don't go directly to her clitoris. It can be uncomfortable because it's very sensitive. Every so often you can flick the hood of her clitoris. See how she responds. Then flick the clitoris directly. Do it more often in between your circular motions if she seems to respond positively. Otherwise, do less often. Some women prefer light touches of the tongue sideways against their clitoris. Get feedback. Don't be shy to ask, do you like this or that better? Let her enjoy the smooth sailing for six to ten minutes before allowing her to reach orgasm.

2. Straight-Shooter—Once you've warmed up your partner, an experienced woman may desire you to suck her clitoris directly, softly at first. Rhythmically until her body moves and or stiffens, then you can increase the intensity of the sucking to match the pace of her movements. Let her reactions lead the way. After she climaxes, start off again slowly, perhaps with circular motions and some intermittent tongue-flicking movements.

3. Finger-flicking—Some women like to be fingered inside at the same time as being licked. You can try gently rubbing her clitoris with a wet finger as well. Keep a steady rhythm so she knows where you are going. Her body will let you know when it's time to speed up. But don't be such a hurry that she doesn't enjoy the ride.

Allow her to climax a few times before switching to a different technique. Try a thumb on the clitoris with a middle finger in the vagina. Move both in and out as you would during intercourse.

4. Licking and Kissing—Feel free to kiss a woman's vagina like you would her lips. Do this in a loving way, and she will open up her heart and body to you more readily. Try long, slow licks, moving downwards from her clitoris to the bottom of her labia (her second lips). Keep a slow, steady rhythm for a while. Let her wiggles and writhing increase her mood. Sometimes she will want you to take her right then and there because she can't wait any longer for penetration.

5. Twin-Hitter—Use your tongue in long steady motions across her clitoris at the same time you twist her nipple and cup her breasts in your hand. Mix and match any number of techniques that gets a positive reaction from your partner. Every woman is a little different, so learn the rhythm she likes. Her mood might change want she wants from day to day. Lighten the pressure. Increase the weight. Discover what works.

6. **Deep-Tonguing**—For some women, they like the feeling of the entire tongue going into their vagina. Sometimes this can be accompanied by a finger or two as well. Of course, most men can't keep this up for a long time, but it's a change of pace and works well with other techniques. You can also use a soft hand over the entire vaginal region for a change-up.

7. Champion Combo—What works one night may not work the next. Men need to be sensitive to a woman's varying moods and body changes. This combination almost always melts your lover. Tease her labia with a few kisses and circular tongue motions. Rub your hands firmly down her inner thighs.

Not too lightly as to tickle her. Not too firmly or rough either. Play with her clitoris with your tongue. Flicking here and there. Licking periodically, you can now place a finger or thumb in her anus. Then put your finger inside her vagina while you're still licking and flicking her clitoris. That should do the trick.

Everyone is different, so explore what she likes. Try each technique above for roughly 3-5 minutes each. Your partner can give you feedback.

Adding Sexual Appetizers

Of course, there is oral stimulation of all kinds beyond fellatio and cunnilingus. It includes a whole range of oral activity. The menu includes:

- bun-biting
- toe-sucking
- ear-licking
- breast-sucking
- body nibbling
- tongue-flicking
- lip-kissing
- scalp massaging

Mix in a few of these sexual appetizers and launch the sparks!

Take a look at oral pleasure as one of the most profound and intimate gestures between two loving individuals. Real success is when two people do the right thing for themselves and simultaneously please their partner. Men and women who see oral sex as an essential part of body awareness are well on their way to increased sexual enjoyment and dependable orgasms.

Having oral sex or not doesn't have to be an all or nothing decision. Compromise may be the simple answer to a tricky issue.

A problem begins when one gender, say the female, reads about the pleasures of oral sex or talks to other women. Perhaps someone had great experiences with a previous partner and now feels resentful about not getting it. Many men wish their spouses would give head the way they've had it in the past. They love their wives, but they miss the pleasure and the intimacy oral sex can bring.

Okay, you're on your own. Good Luck. Practice. Give feedback.

Way to Go! You finished
Chapter 8
Finding Your Oral Intimacy Quotient
(This section can be difficult, so take pride in finishing it!)

CHAPTER 9

GETTING YOUR NEEDS MET

As in most things, communication is the key to success. Good fortune in bed is no different. Talking is no less necessary than other modes of communication, although touching is probably the simplest and most profound way to connect with another human being. However, verbal communication before and after any sexual activity can provide many benefits.

Implementing a variety of communication techniques increases the chances for satisfying results. If words don't come easily to you, try other ways to make your point. Moving your partner's hand where you want it, slowly and gracefully, relays your desire in a transparent manner. An instinctual moaning sound usually gets a repeat performance of something you like.

A verbally-assertive woman has heightened pleasure, and sometimes more orgasms, because she's able to spit out the words: "Honey, can you move a half a millimeter to the left, please?" A simple request said in a loving tone is usually received in that light. Using humor in the right way can increase sensations and help teach your partner at the same time.

Equally important is for you to praise your partner's talent. Then ask for more of a particular delight. Please don't bombard him with a bunch of requests at the same time. He'll panic. Just like you would. Don't say he's a good kisser if he's not. Find something you especially like. If you can't find many reasons to praise your mate, I suggest you reconsider why you're with him in the first place. This goes for men, too.

Variety, skill, and endurance are nice, but who said sexual athletics and prowess are more important than a passion for the lovemaking itself? Men who try to prove themselves by outperforming other men in bed do not make the best partners either.

Unwittingly, many think they're God's gift to women merely because they can keep a hard-on for an hour. A long-standing erect penis is helpful, but that alone does not always satisfy a woman.

Some men pride themselves on size. However, I have found the following expression to be more accurate: "It's not the size of the boat, but the motion of the ocean that counts."

Regarding dimension, though, it's the width of the penis, not the length that counts the most. The girth is more likely to create friction on the clitoris, which is mandatory for an orgasm.

The amusement is in the motion of the ocean!

Have you ever made love to a man who was so well hung that you had second thoughts about going to bed with him? Believe it or not, an over-sized penis can hinder pleasure for a woman unless you take extra time to lubricate properly and he penetrates slowly. Movements must progress from a slow, very deliberate penetration before it proceeds to an inevitable fast-paced crescendo.

Most women can adapt to such a man, of course, and enjoy the results of nature's unexpected blessing. By the way, an un-stretched vagina is roughly four inches long; but it's very elastic. The majority of women can accommodate the man no matter what size he is. The truth of the matter is that serviceability of the penis has nothing to do with size.

The average erect penis is six inches long. Relatively speaking, a short penis can touch the sensitive nerves of a woman's vagina. Since 90% of all nerve fibers are located in the top third of the vaginal canal, length isn't essential for satisfaction. Thickness, if anything, matters more.

If his girth is plentiful enough or his pelvic thrusts are anatomically placed, the clitoris will be stimulated. The woman can determine the angle of this motion, especially if she is on top, which I recommend for those females who have a more difficult time having an orgasm.

This is obvious, but I'm going to say it. Never comment negatively on the size of a man's penis. And, please, don't say how big it is if it's not. Your man has undoubtedly measured his—and he's probably named it, too. And don't ever ask, "Why the name Edna?" if you don't want to hear the answer. Think how hurt you'd be if your lover criticized the size of your breasts, even though you know that has absolutely nothing to do with your sexiness or how physically stimulated you can become.

When your partner comments negatively on your physical appearance, it creates insecurities which can affect performance and diminish the potential for strong orgasms. Be sure to compliment your partner in positive ways to boost confidence, intimacy, and sexual pleasure.

What Are Some Gender Differences?

A man's sexual response is usually triggered by visual things like your hair, breasts, buttocks, or sexy clothing. Don't be confused by this. These things excite him, allowing him to express his love, affection, and desire for you. Women make love with their heart. Men with their eyes. It is common for women to bond through talking. Men connect through activity.

Once an emotional connection has been made, a man can have sex with his heart as well. Visual effects may be less important to her, although most women claim to get excited by their man wearing sexy underwear or nothing at all.

A female turn-on usually involves atmosphere, mood, and how sentimentally attached she is with her mate. Women need to understand another basic thing about men. Most male sexual feelings are centered in the last inch of their penis. This partially explains why males focus on the genital region. That's why they may play with your genitals before you're ready. Just say, "Honey, can you kiss me a little more until I can get warmed up. I love it when we make out first."

Touching his manhood usually gets your mate in the mood for intercourse fast, so time this carefully with what you want. If you go full bore ahead, you may be asking for a quickie. That's fine if that's what you desire. Quickies are great. If you want a more romantic evening, though, go slow. Stroke is penis only occasionally until you're heated up and ready for him to penetrate you.

How To Use Positive Reinforcement

I can't overemphasize this next statement enough. Positive reinforcement, done intermittently, is the most effective way to get more of what you want. Of course, sincerity is important as well. Obviously, you have your unique ways you communicate with your lover to get his attention and praise him.

Here is a list of ways to reinforce the special man or woman in your life:

<u>Verbally:</u>

"Oh, yes, baby, yes."
"You make me so happy."
"Omg, omg, omg..."
"Don't stop!"
"You're magical tonight."
"I love the way you do that."
"I feel so womanly with you."

"Your hands are toasty."

"I feel safe with you."

"Loving you is easy."

Physically:

- A back and neck rub with heated baby oil
- Arm tickling
- Butterfly kisses (eyelash flutters)
- Stroking his or her scalp slowly
- Rubbing hands and fingers
- A full body massage
- A foot massage while watching TV together
- Sucking fingers after eating or before sex
- Sharing a warm bath by candlelight
- Noticeably drawing in his scent
- Love Nibbles (back and butt bites)
- Behind the knee kisses

Unique Ways:

- ☐ Writing poetry
- ☐ Making a homemade card
- ☐ Watching adult videos
- ☐ Posting a personalized note in a fun place
- ☐ Texting a short, sexy message as a prelude
- ☐ Dressing up in satin, lace, or leather
- ☐ Playing an X-rated scavenger hunt

Side Dishes:

It's usually a turn-on to experiment with the following sexual treats:

- Oils and lotions
- Edible Gels
- Vibrators (a variety available)

- French ticklers (for a penis)
- Seductive body paints
- Silk, lace, leather lingerie (turn-on outfits)
- Playful sensory toys
- Sex gadgets (dildos etc.)
- Whipped cream and strawberries
- Edible underwear
- Sex machines
- Ice cubes
- Orgasm balls
- Sex swings (trapeze)
- Anal beads
- Nipple clips
- Electrostimulation
- Sex dolls
- Hot towels
- Cybersex

Explore some of these side dishes. Experimentation is fun. You just might find some activity that blows your socks off!

Be creative. A scavenger hunt, for instance, can be initiated by either party. Start with a simple handwritten note which you strategically placed somewhere you know he'll see it quickly. The sign might read:

"Hello, handsome. Just wanted to show you how much I love you. Here's a coupon for a back massage with hot baby oil. Go to the kitchen for your next message."

Next, you send them to the refrigerator, the couch, anywhere in the house, invariably ending up in the bedroom. Each note tells him how much you love him and why. Humans never tire of hearing flattery. As long as it's true, you can say the same things over and over in different ways.

The note may include a coupon for something he desires, like a five-minute blow job or a foot massage.

The last note may say: "Look under your pillow." Place a small token of your affection or something provocative – like edible underwear – before the games begin. Your gift can be as inexpensive as a card or an expensive gift your partner wasn't expecting. The point is, you've taken the time to be playful while showing your lover how much you care. This fanciful play spills over into the bedroom.

Seduction is Fun and Sexy

Now that you're in the bedroom, seductively and playfully push your lover onto the bed. Offer a glass of wine that happens to be on the nightstand nearby. Start with a kiss or try unbuttoning his shirt, slowly, and continue with each piece of clothing until he's naked. Begin the foreplay until neither of you can prolong the sexual tension a moment longer.

Conversation can be a part of seduction. Talking plays a vital role for both sexes. The strong silent type from the early silver screen era is not considered sexy by women anymore. Of course, most don't want the egocentric chatty guy either. In general, males and females don't want a partner who dotes on their every moment to the point of exaggeration. This constant attention can be perceived as smothering, controlling, or neediness. The real smooth-talking, smooth-acting guy may seem untrustworthy, similar to a salesman whose lines appear rehearsed and not genuine. Other men can nearly talk a woman into a climax with honesty, caring, timing, and personal knowledge of her desires.

Honesty is important in seduction. Don't you love it when your partner says something sweet and meaningful? It can be as simple as this: "I can't get enough of you tonight." Even the quiet type is fine as long as he expresses his loving feelings periodically. It makes sense that the best time to hear some loving remark is before or after sex.

Ways To Match Sexual Appetites

When couples first meet, there's usually an instant chemistry accompanied by a host of sexual sparks. It's easy to fall into a pattern of having sex numerous times a day for weeks, months, and even longer at the start of a blossoming romance.

Once the newness wears off, however, the sparks can become cinders, and that's where the trouble begins. One partner accuses the other of not fulfilling their needs; the other explains the reasons why they can't make love like they used to. Sometimes work, children, family, or health issues get in the way.

There comes a time when couples have to negotiate how many times they want to have sex each week to keep the flames alive. How long the sessions will last on average is another topic to discuss. Some women think it's not worth the trip unless they set aside thirty to forty-five minutes. Others only require seven to twelve minutes. As always, there's a time and a place for quickies, especially if children are involved because you have to grab your dose of sex when you can before there is another disruption in the household.

According to a recent study, the average time spent during sex is about eight minutes. For sexually-active couples, having sex twice a week for roughly fifteen to thirty minutes per session is typical. In general, at least for couples I surveyed, this was an acceptable amount for both parties involved. Of course, a person's age factors in quite a bit because teenagers and twenty-somethings usually require a lot more sex than twice a week. To give credit where it is deserved, there are plenty of fifty-something couples who engage in sexual activity five to six times per week for extended stretches at a time. They've discovered an extra sense of freedom since their children are grown and left the house.

How to Prolong Time in the Sack

Most men figure sex is over once they've ejaculated. Even the total gentleman who takes extra time to make sure a woman climaxes before him can learn a thing or two about a woman's real needs. If you want to have more orgasms, ask for oral or manual stimulation, and be sure to tell him how much pleasure he gives you.

Another method is for the female to remain on top of him even after ejaculation and continue to enjoy more closeness and sometimes more orgasms by rubbing against the warmth of his pelvic body. Even if he's relatively soft, you can learn to climax with the friction of his penis on your clitoris. If he's willing to kiss you and stimulate your breasts, this is twice as easy.

The better you are at making requests, without demanding or belittling, the better the sexual encounter will become. Be subtle. The key is to make your partner feel special during your sexual adventures. To add many delicious minutes to your sexual routine, say things like, "This closeness is nice." By giving honest praise, you can prolong the after-play.

Maybe all you want is to cuddle for a few minutes or to be stroked a little. Once you reassure him that he's the best thing you've ever had, your partner will be more likely to respond to this request rather than turn over and go to sleep. There is a chemical that is released in a man's brain once he's ejaculated. However, that promotes his sleepiness, so be understanding.

Never rate his performance during the afterglow except with an honest exclamation of how you are feeling at that moment: "I feel so relaxed and so loved right now." This is not the time to ask for help painting the house either. Make suggestions during a non-intimidating time, like after reading a magazine article:

"Oh, honey I'd like to try something new in the bedroom tonight." This approach is more effective and will likely get a resounding, "Sure, let's go!"

Your partner probably has already fantasized about trying a few things with you. If you seem interested in sexual experimentation, he'll be more willing to try something that you like as well. Text him the link to an article you read online, and the title alone may entice him to read it. Of course, you have to be receptive to the idea of playing out some of his fantasies unless it's really out of your wheelhouse. What's fair is fair!

The Sexy Afterglow

Usually, but not always, women like to bask in the aftermath of good sex. They want to cuddle, talk, sit together, relax, eat or just hold hands while some men may want to smoke, get up, or just go to sleep. Many people are deficient in this area and almost ruin a perfectly good experience by falling asleep without ever saying "good night." Explain to your partner that you desire at least a few minutes to revel in the afterglow. Stick to a short schedule like you promised.

Agree to spend at least a couple of minutes holding and hugging each other before saying good night. Add minutes whenever possible. Let the stream of consciousness flow after sex where you can share secrets, recall happy memories, tell jokes and connect. Tell each other what's going on in your daily life. A few minutes of acceptance, warmth, and closeness may make all the difference between feeling used and feeling loved. Don't we all need reinsurance of our humanness rather than feeling like a vehicle for sexual release?

Bedroom Philosophy

Think of your bedroom as a personal sanctuary. It is a safe space where you go to relax and recharge your batteries. Therefore, it's important that we take a few moments to talk about bedroom rules. Make sure that your bed is used for two reasons:

1. Sleeping (napping)
2. Pleasure (reading, sex, connecting)

Please don't use the bed as a place to discuss business, problems with the children, or asking for galactic favors. Over time, this behavior triggers a negative response in the bedroom, which is the last place you want to create unpleasant memories.

> # A negative anchor in the bedroom
> # drowns a relationship!

There's a fine line between general talking and troubling discussions. Of course, couples frequently use the bed to discuss the day's events, what they did, who they saw, how people acted, gossip, etc. That's okay. If your conversations turn into logical problem-solving sessions, however, then I suggest you move to the kitchen table to continue your talk.

If you continuously argue in bed, then negative associations begin to take hold. This destructive dynamic will affect you and your partner's attitude toward each other, breaking down the fragments of romance until none remain. Couples inadvertently anchor hostile feelings in the bedroom, which spells disaster for a happy relationship.

Be careful. It doesn't take long before the built-up negative energy begins to spiral out of control. You blame your partner for petty stuff at first while he or she points out how your actions ruined the last three sexual encounters. Nobody wins in the blame game. The first step to recovering the goodness of your relationship is recognition. Be aware that the negative snowball has begun. Stop the bickering cycle in the bedroom. Resolve your issues in another room. (Refer to chapter six for conflict resolution.)

Remember, negativity builds on itself until it stifles your outlook and chips away at the respect, support, and affection you once had for each other. One party eventually disconnects from the relationship. If the bedroom is the primary place you dwell on negative issues, it's bound to have an effect on your overall outlook each time you step into the room. Make your bedroom the most pleasant and upbeat place you possibly can. Revive a positive practice today!

One of the easiest ways to break an unfavorable pattern is to change the looks of your bedroom physically. Move the furniture around. Buy a sexy bedspread or soft and colorful sheets. Add a few houseplants, a new wall decoration, or window dressing. Then sit down and talk to your partner about the new philosophy of the bedroom. Start off by offering a back rub or foot massage to celebrate the new look!

Way to go! You finished

Chapter Nine:
Getting Your Needs Met

Conclusion:
Rekindle, Refresh, Reboot

The gap between thought and action is acceptance of total responsibility for one's gratification. The second revelation is finding your authentic sexual self without depending on your partner for definitive answers. Genuine peace of mind follows the trial and error discovery of what satisfies you and what pleases your partner. Next, it's important to develop an eager action mindset and experiment within your comfort zone.

Living with genuine love and affection is one of the greatest purposes of life. Without it, we merely exist. Life is complicated, so keep your eye on the prize and don't get distracted by fleeting thoughts. Processing this information takes time, but here is a handful of activities to keep you focused:

1st—Write a Relationship Connection Plan (RCP) and evaluate it once or twice a year. Review it around the one-year mark of your first date or wedding anniversary. Consider together. Think separately. Write. What is an RCP?

An RCP is a written statement. An action plan. An announcement. A testimony. An affirmation. It's a signed promise to each other on how you intend to stay emotionally, physically, psychologically, and mentally connected. Clarify your roles today and discuss when it's appropriate to alter them. I urge you to complete your couples plan within the next forty-eight hours while it's fresh in your mind.

2nd—Schedule a monthly F-L-I-E (Focused-Language, Intimacy-Enhanced) session. (Refer to chapter two for the ground rules and goals.) This may be the single most important way to have more peaceful interactions in the future. It's a great way to stay on the same page without expecting the other to read your mind.

3rd—Couples would benefit by establishing their version of the <u>Erotic Discovery Exercise.</u> (Refer to chapters four and seven in this workbook.) Be creative. Use various sources for stimulation. Experiment with household objects, sex toys, or food. Dare to be adventurous!

4th—Schedule your connection time. Call it a standing date if you like. Set up a tentative plan for spending private time together at least twice a month. Decide what time and day work best for you. Set an alert on your cell phone. Include activities you want to do together that rejuvenate you both:

Touch. Talk.
Watch Sunsets.
Love. Laugh. Eat.
Swim. Do Puzzles.
Walk. Play Games.
Hike. Hold Hands.
Look up at the Sky.
See a Movie. Pray.
Go to a Museum.
Listen to Music.
Have a Picnic.
Watch Waves.
Make Love.

Sex is a universal phenomenon, yet it's an individual experience. By completing the activities in this workbook, you have identified many behaviors that benefit your relationship. Additionally, you have discovered how to enhance those areas that needed an upgrade. Of course, there's no substitute for love, affection, and caring. Compatible chemistry is essential for a close emotional connection. The closeness of flesh-to-flesh contact is a physiological trigger that strengthens romantic love. So make the most of it and appreciate your unique partnership.

Let's take a look back at all the progress you've made and a few tips you may have picked up along the way. In the introduction, you learned that striving for the perfect sex scenario often falls short.

Just like Kabrina—who slept with three generations of kings—broke the code for pleasure, you now have the tools to do so yourself. Remember that Kabrina didn't focus on love. She only reacted to the unique personality of each king. She practiced muscle control. She expressed her true self. She enjoyed every nuance and sensation. She relied on her gut instincts. She showed her passion moment to moment.

In the first chapter, you explored a variety of ways to connect with your partner. You also discovered how stable your partnership is when held to a high standard. You learned about a R-I-P-E relationship, which is a healthy state involving respect, intimacy, passion, and emotional support. You also took a quiz to find out where your relationship stands and where it could be headed.

Chapter two helped you gain more intimacy. Through a ten-minute exercise called a Focused-Language Intimacy-Exchange (F-L-I-E), you became more aware of any behaviors blocking intimacy with your partner. The F-L-I-E is where you asked your partner three specific questions:

1. On a scale from 1 to 100, where do you see our intimacy level?
2. Where would you like it to be?
3. What can I do to help move us from a #_____ to a # _____?

Each partner can speak up without the fear of critical remarks (because of the rules). In this way, you feel as though the other person is listening. Without the pressure of immediate feedback, your partner is free to transform, thus ensuring more peaceful interactions. This emotionally-safe activity increases the chances that your partner modifies negative behaviors.

In chapter three, you learned how to foster the right mental mindset. Continue to implement techniques to relate more effectively with your partner. You also learned to create an anchor from an intense emotional experience. For instance, a touch on your partner's wrist may trigger a sexual fantasy. A voice tone and appropriate phrase can become an anchor for a boost of confidence. For an emotional link to remain strong, it needs to be reinforced. Used in public or private, you can trigger a warm fuzzy feeling that is like a secret language known only to the pair of you.

This book discussed the importance of a psychological comfort level as well. The erotic discovery exercises mentioned in chapter four provide a way to focus on one person at a time, which clarifies what works and what doesn't. Feedback is made simple using a one to ten rating system while using words or phrases for specification: faster, slower, rougher, more tender, deeper pressure, lighter touches, etc. In this manner, you can learn about your partner's sexual preferences in a non-intimidating way.

Chapter five covered seven myths and misconceptions both genders commonly have about human sexuality. It discussed the following:

1. A clitoral versus a vaginal orgasm;
2. The types of orgasms;
3. Self-pleasuring;
4. Simultaneous orgasms;
5. Sex and menses,
6. Parenthood; and
7. Aging.

Look to each other for love and affection. Set up a pattern where you put your partner on top of the family totem pole.

Men and women can self-sabotage, unintentionally undermining their partner's pleasure as well. Some lovers are uptight about sex or distracted by thoughts during sexual encounters. Others lack emotional involvement, are too self-conscious about how they look or are embarrassed about how they will sound. Women may be worried about getting pregnant or experiencing feelings of guilt.

Both genders can be anxious or play a spectator role rather than be an active participant. One thing a woman can do for herself, and her partner, is to practice Kegel exercises on a regular basis, which will increase sexual desires. A couple can watch a romantic movie together, offering each other affection squeezes and cuddling, to create bonding.

In chapter six, you learned about cross-gender communication styles and better ways to resolve a conflict. Your partner doesn't need to hear everything that is going on in your head. Your thoughts do not define your identity. They are temporary. Your thoughts are only thoughts. Fleeting. Please realize that you are the thinker.

Lean away from your thoughts when they trouble you. As you learn to separate yourself from your thoughts, you will relax, gain better insights, and make smarter choices. Like an out-of-body experience, pretend you're looking down at yourself and then command your thoughts to move on to something more productive. Additionally in this chapter was a list of do's and don'ts for the bedroom. Couples can inadvertently anchor negative feelings surrounding the bed, which is a major way to ruin a relationship.

Remember to offer grace to your partner each day to solidify the foundation of respect in your relationship. If you become angry with your partner, this emotion may stem from your fear-based ego rather than the actual behavior of the other person. Bitterness is a deadly emotional poison. Anxiety, stress, and past failures also reduce the chances for a positive experience in the bedroom. Fortunately, we can control our behavior and how we react to outside stimuli and negative situations. Make forgiveness a priority. Holding onto anger and resentment is a death sentence for any partnership. You might as well start digging two graves.

Chapter seven reviewed compatible chemistry and kissing. You took a quiz to determine your psychological comfort level with your partner. We periodically forget the simple joys of spending half a day in bed: stroking, cuddling, kissing, petting, and loving each other. Remember, sex is like food. Sometimes we crave a hot dog; other nights we want a seven-course meal. Communicate what you want when you want it, and there's a greater chance for success. Again, your partner can't read your mind.

Chapter eight provided you with detailed information about oral sex. It offered specific ways to overcome obstacles for oral gratification. Awaken the dormant natural energy within. You may have learned a few new techniques to try. Perhaps you had previous negative experiences because of an insensitive or uninformed partner. Now that you've found a new lover, give oral sex a fair shot. Use it to enhance your lovemaking sessions. Dare to break the barriers. Have faith that you can explore your instinctual side with someone you love. Be a sexual adventurer, and you'll taste the ecstasy of erotic paradise!

Chapter nine wrapped up numerous topics related to getting your needs met. Obviously, our emotional and energetic sexual supply can change day-to-day for many reasons, including fatigue, hunger, pain, health, mood, pregnancy, medication interference, and the use of alcohol or drugs. Some of these barriers are difficult to control, but sometimes a good night's sleep is all it takes to remedy problems from the day before. On these days, the best approach is to be completely honest with your lover: "My head is not in the right space for sex today, babe. I'll let you know when I'm ready." Then follow-up as soon as possible.

When considering the frequency of foreplay and sex, what's adequate for one person may not be enough for another. Additionally, your needs vary from one day to the next. Communicate openly about how you're feeling and then be willing to compromise to fulfill your partner's desires.

Breathing deeply is important, especially during crescendos of sex. Oxygen in our lungs stimulates our senses. So breathing fully and rhythmically enhances your sexual pleasure. If your mouth is slightly opened and your wrists and knees are bent, you will automatically be more relaxed. Fill your chest and lungs first, filling your abdomen last when inhaling. When exhaling, you reverse the process. Air leaves your lower area first and then the upper cavity. Proper breathing, practiced daily, will keep you grounded and allow for a full appreciation of your physical senses.

Sex sounds are natural. Like breathing, making noises lets your partner know you are an eager participant. As you let out grunts and groans, you exchange energy, letting the other person know the depth and tempo of rhythm you prefer with each new release. Vocalizing instinctive sounds strikes an emotional inner chord, letting your partner know you are delighted by his or her actions.

For great results, experiment with a variety of positions during sex: frontal, sideways, rear entry, and astride. Even after years of having sex with the same partner, you can discover new variations. Try different tilts and angles of penetrations for new sensations. Vary leg positions (open, closed, bent, straight, crossed, and overlapping). Some physically demanding positions are hardly worth the trip except to satisfy your curiosity while others may become a favorite. And remember, ladies, you can always adjust your cylinder to his piston—especially when you are on top—which gives you greater control of thrusting rhythms for a better chance to reach your climax.

A man's emotional power and personal energy can often awaken a woman's passion. At the same time, her imagination and stamina can take both lovers to greater heights. Passion is reciprocated best when partners are not thinking about the past or the future. Relish each moment as it unfolds.

**Sex is like food.
Sometimes you want a seven-course meal.
Sometimes you crave a hot dog!**

Dare to Awaken Your Sexual Core!

Look back over your answers as a way to review what you have learned. Do this again in six months to refresh your memory. Continue to practice the skills and activities in this workbook to gain extra brownie points. That said, you will also reap the rewards of a satisfying and peaceful romantic love life.

Sextastic! Improve your Love Life in Seven Weeks is your personal guide for accepting your sacred sexuality and building a strong foundation for a long amorous partnership. Discovering your sexual awareness brings emotional treasures into other areas of your life. Now that you've completed the exercises in this book, you will be able to open up lines of communication, tap into your creativity, concentrate better, relate to a higher degree, express your desires, and love to the fullest.

Congratulations! You've completed seven weeks of self-discovery and interactive partnering exercises. Remember, love is the best aphrodisiac. Let your heart and natural instincts be your guide. With the techniques and tools you've learned, you will enjoy a lifetime of enhanced love, sex, romance, and intimacy. Good luck on your unique romantic adventure. Super job, couples!

EXCELLENT WORK!

For more helpful tips, please visit my website for
information on personal transformation,
romance, parenting, and inner wisdom.
(My ebooks help men, too.)

https://wisewords4women.com/

About the Author

A well-qualified professional, Janalee Beck holds a Master's degree in English from Arizona State University. She has been an adjunct faculty member, a social worker, a licensed Legal Document Preparer, and has held an advanced designation as a financial planner (CRPC ®). Beck is a published author, has shared her insights through seminars, and supports other women through networking and writing ebooks.

In 1993, Avon Books (NY) published her first book, *How to Have Multiple Orgasms*, about female sexuality. The book is more down-to-earth than the title suggests. It sold over 56,000 copies and was translated into Spanish and Chinese. Beck now shares her secrets and bedroom philosophy with the next generation as well as others who want to spread their romantic wings later in life.

As founder of Wisdomality Enterprises, Janalee promotes her website— wisewords4women.com—which is devoted to elevating the inner power of women to direct their life path with confidence. Her self-help ebooks on romance, transformation, and parenting offer practical ways to create an environment where readers learn about personal growth, forgiveness, spiritual exploration, positive reinforcement, authentic communication, and humor.

She has two millennial children, Grant and Janelle, who are treasured pieces of her heart walking around in the world. She makes her home in Scottsdale, Arizona and enjoys traveling, swimming, piano, fascial stretch therapy, earthing, playing poker, reading, meditation, games, and visiting family.

Suggested Reading List

1. *You Just Don't Understand* by Deborah Tannen, 2013
2. *He said, She said: Women, Men, and Language* by Dr. Deborah Tannen, 2008
3. *Instant Rapport*, by Michael Brooks, 1990
4. *Frogs Into Princes: Neuro Linguist Programming* by Bandler and Grinder, 1979
5. *The New Earth: Awakening to Your Life's Purpose* by Eckhart Toll, 2007
6. *The Power of Now: A Guide to Spiritual Enlightenment* by Eckhart Tolle, 2004
7. *Excuse Me, Your Life is Waiting* by Lynn Grabhorn, 2003
8. *The Prophet* by Kahil Gibran, 1923
9. *The Psychology of Man's Possible Evolution* by P.D. Ouspensky, 1973
10. *The Hite Report: A Nationwide Study of Female Sexuality* by Shere Hite, 1970
11. *Deliberately Living: The Discovery and Development of Avatar* by Harry Palmer and Nestor Sanchez, 1994
12. *The Seat of the Soul: 25th Anniversary with a Study Guide* by Gary Zukav, 2014
13. *The Last Lecture* by Randy Pausch, 2010
14. *As a Man Thinketh: The Original Masterpiece, Updated For Today*, by James Allen, 2016
15. *Earthing: The Most Important Health Discovery Ever!* by Clinton Ober and Dr. Stephen T. Sinatra M.D., 2014
16. *My Voice Will Go with You: The Teachings of Milton H. Erickson* by Sidney Rosen, 1991

17. *The Tipping Point* by Malcolm Gladwell, 2002

18. *Ask and It is Given: Learning to Manifest Your Desires* by Ester and Jerry Hicks, 2003

19. *Siddhartha* by Herman Hesse, 1951, 2015

20. *The Untethered Soul:The Journey Beyond Yourself* by Michael A. Singer, 2007

21. *Ask And You Will Succeed: 1001 Ordinary Questions to Create Extraordinary Results* by Ken D. Foster, 2003

22. *The 7 Habits of Highly Effective People* by Stephen R. Covey, 1989

23. *The Art of Happiness* by The Dalai Lama XIV, 1998

24. *The Road Less Traveled* by Scott Peck, 1978

25. *The Alchemist* by Paulo Coelho, 1988

26. *Embraced by the Light* by Betty J. Eadie, 1992

27. *The Eagle and the Rose* by Rosemary Altea, 1995

28. *Stumbling On Happiness* by Daniel Gilbert, 2006

29. *The Magic of Faith* by Joseph Murphy, (1954) 2008

30. *The Elegance of a Hedgehog* by Muriel Barberry, 2006

31. *Tantra: The Cult of the Feminine* by André Van Lysebeth, 1995

32. *Blink: The Power of Thinking without Thinking* by Malcolm Gladwell, 2005

33. *The Four Agreements: A Practical Guide to Personal Freedom* by Miguel Ruiz, 1997

Made in United States
Troutdale, OR
12/30/2025

45002191R20099